I0109691

PRAISE FOR
STAY RELEVANT

"*Stay Relevant* is a timely and practical guide for anyone navigating the realities of today's workplace. Drawing on decades of experience in executive recruitment and career coaching, Chris Flakus and Candace Moody deliver a framework that is both honest and empowering. Their focus on mindset, skillset, and mirrorset gives professionals at every stage of their career the tools to adapt, grow, and thrive in an environment shaped by disruption, technology, and generational change. This book is not just about staying employed—it's about staying valuable, fulfilled, and future-ready. A must-read for professionals ready to reinvent themselves and for leaders who want to build resilient teams."

—STACEY C. LANE, CEO, Staffmark Group

"Chris Flakus combines decades of leadership and recruitment expertise with Moody's coaching wisdom to create a must-read guide. This book equips you to conquer workplace change with practical, timeless strategies."

—DELORES PASS KESLER, former CEO
and chairman, AccuStaff, Inc.

"Practical, courageous, and deeply human, this book feels like a trusted mentor walking beside you through every stage of life and career. With heartfelt wisdom from Chris Flakus and Candace Moody, it invites you to pause, reflect, and take bold steps toward growth—whether you're starting out, reinventing yourself, or leading others. A must-have for recruiters, coaches, and HR and talent leaders, it's not just a career guide; it's a reminder that resilience, purpose, and intention can transform both your work and your life."

—ANGELA LOVE, founder and principal, The Daymark Group

"I've always believed that mental toughness is doing the best you can with what you have, wherever you are. That's exactly what *Stay Relevant* teaches but for your career. Chris Flakus doesn't sugarcoat the reality that the workplace has changed dramatically. Instead, he gives you a step-by-step system to adapt, grow, and thrive no matter what comes your way. The winner's mindset isn't just about sports; it's about staying relevant in a world that's constantly evolving. If you're tired of feeling stuck or passed over, this book is your playbook for taking back control of your professional future."

—**ALAN STEIN, JR.**, author and performance coach

"Having worked with Chris Flakus for more than twenty years, I find it comes as no surprise to see that he and Candace Moody have written a powerful and relevant book. Chris is the best of the best, and *Stay Relevant* brings his expert insight on thriving in today's fast-changing workplace."

—**RACHELLE GOTTLIEB**, HR executive

"I hire thousands of people every year, and the ones who thrive all share one trait. They never stop adapting. Chris captures this perfectly with his core question, 'Would you hire you?' If that makes you uncomfortable, read this book. The twelve-week system works because it's built on real experience placing real people in real jobs. Chris understands that staying relevant isn't about age. It's about mindset."

—**DWIGHT COOPER**, executive chairman,
Hueman People Solutions

Stay
Relevant

Stay
Relevant

CONQUER WORKPLACE CHANGE
AT EVERY PHASE OF YOUR CAREER

Chris Flakus
with Candace Moody

FC

FAST
COMPANY
Press

This publication is designed to provide accurate and authoritative information in regard to the subject matter covered. It is sold with the understanding that the publisher and author are not engaged in rendering legal, accounting, or other professional services. Nothing herein shall create an attorney-client relationship, and nothing herein shall constitute legal advice or a solicitation to offer legal advice. If legal advice or other expert assistance is required, the services of a competent professional should be sought.

Fast Company Press
New York, New York
www.fastcompanypress.com

Copyright © 2026 Chris Flakus and Candace Moody

All rights reserved.

Thank you for purchasing an authorized edition of this book and for complying with copyright law. No part of this book may be reproduced, stored in a retrieval system, used for training artificial intelligence technologies or systems, or transmitted by any means, electronic, mechanical, photocopying, recording, or otherwise, without written permission from the copyright holder.

This work is being published under the Fast Company Press imprint by an exclusive arrangement with Fast Company. Fast Company and the Fast Company logo are registered trademarks of Mansueto Ventures, LLC. The Fast Company Press logo is a wholly owned trademark of Mansueto Ventures, LLC.

Distributed by Greenleaf Book Group

For ordering information or special discounts for bulk purchases, please contact Greenleaf Book Group at PO Box 91869, Austin, TX 78709, 512.891.6100.

Design and composition by Greenleaf Book Group
Cover design by Greenleaf Book Group
Cover image used under license from ©Adobestock.com
Art: Genildo Ronchi

Publisher's Cataloging-in-Publication data is available.

Print ISBN: 978-1-63908-171-4

eBook ISBN: 978-1-63908-172-1

To offset the number of trees consumed in the printing of our books, Greenleaf donates a portion of the proceeds from each printing to the Arbor Day Foundation. Greenleaf Book Group has replaced over 50,000 trees since 2007.

Printed in the United States of America on acid-free paper

26 27 28 29 30 31 32 33   10 9 8 7 6 5 4 3 2 1

This book is dedicated to the memory of Guy Cuddihee—
thanks for taking a chance on me all those years ago.
Wish we could have toasted this book together!

CONTENTS

A NOTE TO THE READER

This book is a collaborative effort between me, Chris Flakus, CEO of CSI Companies, and Candace Moody, writer and career coach. The book is written in the first person, "I" (Chris), but I will be quoting Candace and using many of Candace's experiences with her own clients throughout the book. You will notice that at times I will be speaking from two very different perspectives and work histories—me as a CEO and Candace as a one-on-one coach. Nevertheless, we both share a common call to help others stay relevant in the workplace. When I went out looking for books that considered both an executive recruiter's and a career coach's approach to preparing today's aging job seekers and employees, I kept coming up short. I decided I needed to write a book that covered all the bases, so I called on my colleague Candace for both her writing and coaching expertise.

Together we have a combined fifty-plus years' experience in this area.

I have been working in recruitment for thirty years. For the past twenty years I have worked in various roles at CSI, serving eight years as the COO and the past three as the CEO. For over a decade, I was directly involved in executive searches, placing hundreds of candidates in roles where candidates earned 75,000 to 300,000 dollars a year.

Candace is a writer with over twenty-five years of experience in career coaching and workforce development. She's been a columnist for the *Florida Times-Union* and the *Jacksonville Business Journal*, writing about employment and career transition. Her husband's career as a naval aviator took her to Boston, Italy, San Diego, and Norfolk, Virginia. She knows a thing or two about how to adjust to a new location and job. As a military spouse for the first twenty years of her marriage, she had to start over every three or four years in a completely new city where she had no contacts, no context, and she had to reinvent herself. She had to figure out what was going to be relevant to a whole new set of employers, and that reinventing herself gave her the confidence that it can be done. She went back to graduate school and earned her MBA when she was forty.

Candace often says, "When you realize—and admit—you're not the smartest person in the room anymore, then you have the opportunity to grow. When you're not so busy defending your position, you have the ability to open up to new possibilities." Because she has been through it so many times and I have seen so many of my clients go through it, we have a lot of empathy for those embarking on this journey. We know all too well how painful and scary it can be. We also know that anyone, if they're willing, can make the necessary changes and learn the skills required to stay relevant.

I hope that you will benefit from hearing both what recruiters (and by proxy their clients) are looking for and what executive coaches are advocating, so you can stay relevant, age-proof your career by keeping up with the rapidly changing work environment, and set yourself up for success.

And one more matter of business: For the purposes of protecting the identities of clients and employees, I have changed names and identifying characteristics throughout the book. But the spirit of the story remains.

—**Chris Flakus**

WOULD YOU HIRE YOU?

A couple of years ago Greg, a local executive, came to see me. Like many executives out of work, Greg came to CSI Companies because it is a trusted partner to Fortune 500 companies providing strategic guidance in areas of staffing, technology, and managed workforce. Greg thought, as many executives looking for work do, "I'll show up and Chris will hook me up with a job." Little did Greg know that I work with clients *to find the best fit for positions*—jobs aren't always guaranteed. Contrary to what many executives like Greg think, I am not in the field of "handing out jobs" to executives who show up at my office. I try to match the best executives to the culture of the organizations and clients CSI supports.

Prior to coming to me, Greg had been looking for work on his own for over a year, wasn't having much success, and was at a loss for why. He had a great career as an executive—in fact, he did so well, he thought he could go out on his own and work as a consultant. However, he quickly found the work he did as an executive didn't translate into being a consultant, and he was running out of money and time. After a few years of bouncing around and trying to make a go of it on his own in multiple fields, including the nonprofit sector, Greg decided it was time to, in his own words, "jump back into the 'world of work.'"

Easier said than done.

Greg had been out of the corporate world for over six years and a lot had changed in that time. He had chosen to leave a C-suite position. Even though he once had been a Chief Operating Officer (COO) and been making good money, he was neither qualified to "jump" back in nor able to earn what he had hoped. He was extremely motivated to work and earn (given his depleted funds), so he couldn't figure out why organizations didn't want to hire him. He thought he was looking in the right places—for jobs at the same level that he left and above, senior VPs and officer-level opportunities in his area.

Dressed in a suit that was in style more than a decade ago, he plopped down in my office and immediately launched into a speech that I could recite from memory. I had heard the same version of this very speech many times from people just like Greg: "Chris, I don't get it! I just don't! I know I can provide real value. I have had so much experience. Anybody would want me! Look at all I have accomplished in my career."

Now, you would think Greg might feel a bit humbled after a year of unsuccessful job-seeking. But executives like Greg aren't too quick to eat humble pie. They're usually shocked, dumbfounded, even annoyed that anyone wouldn't want to hire them on the spot.

"Chris, just look at my experience! Look at my success six years ago. People know my name. I was in the *Business Journal*. They're crazy not to want me."

We were not off to a great start. As I sat and listened to Greg's monologue, I couldn't help but think: *This guy is the same age as me. We have similar experiences. But I've stayed in the working world and he hasn't. And I am coachable, and this guy doesn't seem to be. This isn't going to be easy . . .*

I knew I had to be as direct as possible. "Let's take a step back, Greg, and talk about the job market today versus how it was when you left six years ago. *Would you hire you?*"

Greg stood up and left, clearly shocked I didn't just "hand him a position."

Fast forward to three months later. Greg walked through my office door, sat down, and admitted defeat. "All right," he said. "Let's talk. I need help. What can I do? What am I missing?"

I repeated what I had tried to ask Greg months earlier: "Let's just talk about what's going on in the world. Let's talk about the relevance of your experience. Yes, you've sat out for six years. What's changed in six years? *And would you hire you* to come in and be a COO or an executive VP of a company? Would you seriously hire you if you'd been out of work for six years?"

Unfortunately, Greg didn't get it. He couldn't see what I wanted him to recognize. The problem wasn't with all the organizations that weren't willing to hire him; the problem was that Greg was unwilling to put in the work to stay relevant in the workplace. Because he had spent twenty-five years in the workforce, he figured organizations owed him something.

After Greg left the office, I vowed to figure out a way to help others see what Greg couldn't—that there are things that he could do to help him find success, not just in his current job search, but throughout the life of his career.

• • •

Candace faced similar issues with clients who came to her for advice. These were people who have been with their companies for several years, sometimes decades, and who can't figure out why they are passed over for promotions. They've hit a glass ceiling and aren't sure why.

Candace recalls one client in particular. Brooke was a smart, kind, Energizer bunny of a woman who was amazing at any task she set her mind to. She was a wonderful employee who received excellent reviews and high praise but was always passed over for promotions. Brooke had been hustling for fifteen years to do everything she could at the level that she was at. No matter what she did, she wasn't considered management material. When she came to Candace she was in despair.

Brooke sat in Candace's office and cried, "They love me, but why won't they love me in a management position?" Why couldn't she reach that elusive "next level"? Candace did some digging around and discovered something: Unbeknownst to Brooke, she had made a name for herself as the "office mom." She was the one who took all the notes, arrived early and made the coffee, baked cupcakes for meetings, and bustled around during meetings clearing people's plates and refilling their cups. Brooke didn't understand; no matter how pleasant she was and how hard she tried, she kept getting turned down for higher level management positions because she'd positioned herself as a cheerful assistant. The truth was that she'd locked herself into a role that no one saw as the next generation of leadership. Her own helpful nature was holding her back.

Greg's and Brooke's stories aren't unique. Both of their scenarios are replayed in recruitment and coaching offices all over the country every day. Many people who are eager to be hired and/or promoted within their own company can't figure out why they are overlooked.

Chances are, if you're reading this book, this could be you too. Over the course of your career, have you:

- been passed over for a promotion, but don't know why?
- felt disconnected from your company's culture?
- wondered why you're not getting callbacks on applications or interviews?

- considered whether, in all honesty, you might hesitate to hire or promote you?

Candace and I have heard the answer to these questions thousands of times and it's usually some form of: "Yes! Of course I should get the offer! My skills and experience are totally in line with what they're looking for!"

But dig deeper, and it becomes clear a key reason is missing. It's time to address the (Older) Elephant in the Room.

THE OLDER ELEPHANT IN THE ROOM (AGEISM)

Often, when clients come to me for help finding a position or come to Candace for coaching, they have a list of complaints—about the companies they worked for, the culture, or their own frustration with not getting the jobs or promotions they desire. Even though many clients (and companies) don't want to admit it, or necessarily confront the issue head on, ageism is a factor, especially for older candidates.

When you get stuck, it's hard to figure out from the place you're standing why you can't move on. I hear it a lot: "I'm still doing all the right things that I have been doing for ten, fifteen, or twenty years." Unfortunately, what you can't see is that while you were standing still, the world kept moving. Albert Einstein is commonly attributed as having said, "You can't solve a problem with the same level of thinking that got you there." And you can't get yourself unstuck by using the same thinking that got you stuck in the first place. The truth is that the longer you've been around, the more you need to rethink how you do things. Often people who have been in the workforce for ten to twenty years believe they are being discriminated against because of their "age." In my mind, ageism is a proxy for the "fixed mindset" or what Candace and

I call a "stuck mindset." Have you ever found yourself thinking "I don't get it; this is how I have always done things," or "this worked for me in the past"? If so, that's an indication that a "stuck" or "fixed" mindset is probably holding you back from future success.

I know how hard it is to get unstuck and remain relevant—now more than ever. The workplace has changed. Today, teams are made up of Boomers, Gen X, Xennials, Millennials, and Gen Z either working side-by-side or remotely via Zoom or Microsoft Teams. Part-time, full-time, freelancer, gig, and crowdsourced workers must all adapt to new market demands as hierarchies are dismantled in favor of new, collaborative-based structures. The old way of conducting "business as usual" is hardly usual and doesn't look like business. These days, it's pretty rare to see a group of business suits headed to the boardroom carrying a sheaf of papers. Since COVID, the workplace is virtually unrecognizable—we have generational dynamics and cultural shifts, not to mention post-pandemic changes. Forget about being out of the workforce for six years—you're out of touch if you've been out for six months. There's no choice but to keep up.

If you want to get unstuck, and not feel limited by your age, you'll need to change your thinking and age-proof your career by adopting the mindsets, skillsets, and what we call mirrorsets (abilities that help you self-reflect) that develop your:

- Coachability—the ability to receive instruction and adopt a beginner's mindset

- Adaptability—the ability to work in a low-structure environment or one with lots of ambiguity

- Curiosity—an openness to admit you might be wrong or that there might be a better way

- Ability to Receive Feedback—an openness to accept and apply constructive criticism

- Values-Based Thinking—the ability to align your beliefs and non-negotiables with the company's culture

- Excellence—understanding how to identify your niche and add value

- Story—the ability to view your role, experience, participation, level of commitment, attitude, behaviors, and results through an employer lens and manage your own expectations

- Sharpness—the ability to keep up with constant changes to technology, social media platforms, and advances in AI

- First Impression—understanding why your image may be holding you back and how to change it

- Authenticity—being able to truly be yourself, express your ideas, thoughts, and values, and live your purpose within a company's culture (and not feel like you are compromising yourself or feeling like a fraud or imposter)

- Brand—the ability to tell your story to the world and succinctly state who you are, what value you bring, and how you'll serve the organization

- Culture—the ability to fit in with a young workforce and work with—and especially for—someone much younger than yourself and still be comfortable

OUR PROMISE TO YOU

Candace and I have helped thousands of job seekers access training and build meaningful careers. With this book, you can gain a new mindset, skillset, and what we call *mirrorset* that will set you up for success in just three months. These tools will help you stay relevant and in high demand throughout the life of your career.

Be prepared for some hard work and some tough talk. We're not sugarcoating our advice because it serves no one to hold back the truth. I am going to be direct and prescriptive, but I am also going to be empathetic and supportive. My hope isn't to discourage you from going after your goals, but to give you a better understanding of yourself and the expectations of the current workforce.

This book is broken down into three sections—mindset, skillset, and mirrorset (skills that help you understand how others perceive you). Each section should take about a month to complete. Throughout, I will give you weekly assessments and tasks to keep you relevant, hirable, promotable, coachable, and desirable. While anyone can complete these skillsets in three months, it's more important to work within a timeframe that is right for you. Then we hope you'll revisit these chapters at other points throughout your career.

WHAT IS THE STORY YOU WANT TO TELL?

In the novel *The Art of Fielding*, a young baseball coach says he knew coaching could be reduced to this: "All you had to do was look at each of your players and ask yourself: What story does this guy wish someone would tell him about himself? And then you told the guy that story."[1] I hope to tell you the story of what you wish someone would say about you. What is the story of the career you envision? What is the story you want others to tell about you? Three months from now? Three years from now? Ten years from now? What needs to change to make that story happen? Together we will find the answers to help you take charge of writing your story. And if the story you're telling right now isn't so great, I want to help you change it to one that will make you more marketable and more relevant, but more importantly, happier, healthier, and more confident.

I have seen these methods and tools work again and again, and I am confident they will work for you no matter what life brings. I can't guarantee there won't be layoffs or recessions, economic or industry changes, health or familial changes, but with these tools you can handle whatever comes your way throughout your career.

INITIAL ASSESSMENT

Grab a notebook and take a few moments to reflect. I suggest using the same notebook (or write it down here in the book or in the downloadable PDF at chrisflakus.com) so you can track your progress over the next three months.

It's possible that one or more of these prompts will be true, so feel free to check off more than one in each category.

1. If you're looking for work or a new position, are any of these things true for you?

    °   I send out resumes to every company/posting I think will fit but get nothing but rejection letters (if I'm lucky).

    °   I get invited to interviews that I think went well, but never seem to make the cut.

    °   I'm trying to make contacts at companies, but I can't get people to return my calls.

    °   I attend networking events and meet lots of people, but they never seem to have time to connect again afterward.

    °   I feel like I'm so much more qualified than people who are getting the offers I want.

      ° I've applied for several new positions/promotions within my company, but never got selected.

2. How would you rate your ability to self-reflect and receive constructive criticism?

      ° I don't really listen to people who want to give me advice when they're less experienced or junior to me.

      ° I ask for constructive feedback, but most people just use it as an excuse to tell me what I'm doing wrong.

      ° I listen to feedback, but I follow my own judgment in the end.

      ° I'm open to hearing how I can improve.

      ° I actively seek out advice that will help me grow.

3. Do you have an accurate idea of how people perceive you?

      ° I don't worry much about what other people think; I'm confident in who I am.

      ° I can tell by the way people react to me what they think of me.

      ° I want to be judged on my performance; not how much people like me.

      ° My work persona is different than how I am as a friend, spouse, or parent, so I worry more about being loved at home than at work.

      ° No one complains, so I'm probably doing fine—if they had a problem with me, they'd let me know.

      ° I worry about what people say or think about me, but I'm afraid to ask.

      ° I've asked for honest feedback, and people seem to think I'm doing fine.

- I have regular conversations with people I trust and take their feedback to heart.

4. Where do you hope to see yourself three months from now after you have implemented the methods and tools from this book? (Check all that apply.)

    - I'll get credit for what I know and appreciation for the work I do.

    - I'll get a great job offer.

    - I'll get a promotion or a great assignment/project.

    - I'll be too essential to my company to be considered for a layoff or urged to retire early.

    - I'll be confident enough to take bigger risks.

    - I'll be able to make more and better connections at work or within my industry.

    - I'll be considered for leadership positions at work or in my community.

    - People will listen to me more.

    - I'll fit in better with my team.

    - I'll be a better manager.

    - I'll be more confident about my skills, experience, and career trajectory.

    - I won't be worried about the future; I know I'll be okay.

5. What on a scale of one to five, is your level of commitment to making necessary changes to achieve the goal(s) you listed above?

    - One: I'll make changes only if I'm sure they'll get the results I want.

- ° Two: I'll think about making changes after I've considered the risks and benefits.

- ° Three: I'm not yet sure I will commit.

- ° Four: I'm open to making changes.

- ° Five: I am committed to making changes that will help me grow.

MONTH ONE

Mindset Practices

Once your mindset changes, everything on the
outside will change along with it.

—**Steve Maraboli,** athlete, coach, speaker, and
author of *Unapologetically You*

INTRODUCTION TO MINDSET

Chances are, if you bought this book, you know you already need to change something. Whatever you've been doing isn't working. I think the first thing that needs to change is your mindset. What do I mean by mindset? Carol Dweck, author of *Mindset: The New Psychology of Success*, defines a mindset as a set of beliefs that define what you can and can't do. According to Dweck, a person either has a "fixed" or "growth" mindset. Those with a fixed mindset hold the belief their intelligence, talents, and abilities are set in stone—and no matter what they do, they can't change them. Conversely, those with a growth mindset believe that with effort, practice, perseverance, and drive, one can learn and develop the skills and traits required to achieve their goals.[1] I am not here to convince you that you're broken or that you have a fixed mindset. I'm here to help you do what you need to do and to give you a system, a way of making changes that will make a difference. I believe it's possible for everyone to adopt a growth mindset and develop the skills they need to thrive.

In the Introduction, I asked the question: *Would you hire you?* Chances are you would. But the workforce is evolving—and that means you're going to have to evolve right along with it. However, most of us can't perceive that these changes are happening. We *think* we're changing, adapting, and keeping up with the times, but are we? The problem when trying to stay relevant is that most of us don't realize we've started to lag.

The biggest mindset shift starts right here—by recognizing that you don't have all the answers. You don't know what you don't know. What you probably *do* know is that it's time to upgrade your skills and put yourself out there. It's time to open yourself to learning something new.

Your mindset makes a difference. Compare the smug *Yeah, I'd hire/ promote me*, to the more realistic *I, like everyone around me, need to constantly be improving to remain relevant*. It doesn't seem like much, but it's a major shift that adds self-awareness to your self-confidence. And that opens the door to change.

For a moment I want you to put yourself in the shoes of a prospective employer or recruiter. I want you to see the candidates' resumes and the interviews they review. Nine out of ten times, when I tell someone they aren't going to be hired, it's not because they're not a "good fit" for the company. It's because they're competing with a new generation of really attractive alternatives. The reality is these candidates are up against go-getters who are just out of college, hungry and ready to learn; they are prepared to go above and beyond. They are current with all the latest technology and trends. What they lack in experience, they make up for in a willingness to learn and take direction—in other words, they have a learner's mindset.

Charles walked into my office ready to be hired. He was in his late fifties and had a ton of experience working in executive-level positions. He was unhappy in his current role and hoped that I would help. We scheduled a thirty-minute, in-person meeting. He shook my hand, took a seat, and then started talking. *And talking. And talking . . . and . . . talking.* I sat there watching him the whole time. He spent the first twenty-two minutes of our thirty minutes together telling me everything he'd done, how much success he'd had, and how frustrated he was that he wasn't where he thought he should be. In his mind, he believed he should be the CEO of a company—*any* company. He was that good. He even went as far as to say, "I could do any job here at CSI, including your job."

Yeah, he was *that guy*. We've all had to endure some insufferable person at a meeting or gathering, someone who felt they could literally explain everything to you—including your own job—without ever having spent a day in the position. As mindboggling as it sounds, it happens every day in recruitment offices all over the world. Somewhere, right now, someone is explaining to a potential employer/boss how much better they would be at doing *their* job.

It's not a strategy I recommend.

It's a major turnoff and completely insulting. But let's pretend for a second that he *could* do my job, and that he would run circles around me. There is always the chance. But I would never know or see that because Charles spent so much time talking about *where he'd been* and *what he'd done* that we never had the chance to talk about what he wanted to do in the future. A better use of our time would have been if he could tell me where he fit in the market *right now*, and how his skills and experience could be leveraged to improve outcomes in the *future*. He could have talked about all the ways he was trying to learn innovative technologies or keep abreast of new challenges in his specific industry.

Instead, in the eight remaining minutes of our one-on-one, I had to explain to him that where he was currently and what it was that he was trying to do with his career now was impossible, especially given the competition. That was hard for Charles to hear. No one wants to hear that, instead of climbing the mountain, they are sliding down the backside of the hill. I offered him a mid-level position as an option, and he left my office angry and frustrated.

It's a tough pill to swallow: At one point in your career, you were that up-and-comer who everybody wanted to hire, and now you're basically being shown the door on your way out. Maybe you, too, are someone who has a ton of experience; it may feel like a step down to enter a mid-level position. Frankly, the odds were that Charles would struggle to succeed even at that level, knowing what I did about him from our short meeting.

FOCUS ON THE FUTURE, NOT THE PAST.

Candace sees this struggle in her coaching practice, too. "I see a lot of people who come to me focused on the past. The reality is employers only care about the future." When coaching mid-career professionals, she's spoken to many who want to step out and go into consulting. "I'm so smart and I have so much experience, I need to go out on my own," they say. And for many of them, it's the right idea. But they need to change their mindset first from candidate to consultant.

One way to make that change (in both your mind and a company's) is to change the way you talk about what you do. Candace recommends that clients put a proposal together, instead of a resume. "A resume talks all about what you have done. A proposal, in a consultant's world, talks about what you will do and what you can do, and it's targeted specifically for that client or employer." The same applies to job interviews or in a recruitment office—think of what type of "proposal" you can offer. Then shift from *Look what I have done!* to:

What can I do for you? What problem needs to be solved?

How can my current level of experience and my willingness to adapt best serve you, your goals, and your culture?

What characteristics are you (the employer) and the company in the most need of at this moment in time?

POTENTIAL TRUMPS EXPERIENCE.

The ideal candidate will come to me having done their homework. They might do research into current and coming trends. They might highlight specific changes in the industry and show the recruiter or employer how their skills and experience can address those changes. They might even come to the table with a list of workshops or classes they have taken recently, conferences they've attended, or books they've read that have influenced them in how they approach people, problems, or possibilities.

Let's move from business to sports for a moment. When recruiters pursue athletes, they are typically looking for *potential*. Tom Brady is the perfect example. Brady was not a first-round draft pick; he wasn't even the second. In fact, he wasn't selected until the sixth round of the NFL draft. He was eventually the 199th pick in 2000. When he was drafted, what he offered was "potential"—a willingness to learn, grow, and improve. Indeed, when he first headed out on the practice field, he wasn't getting any opportunities with the ball. He went to a coach and asked how he could possibly stand out if he only got the ball once during practice. His coach told him to work hard even when no one was looking. When he got his time with the ball, even if it was for only a second, he needed to make sure it was the best damned second of the practice.

And that is exactly what Tom Brady did. He was tenacious. When he had an opportunity with the ball, he did the best he could. He didn't offer excuses. He didn't go to a coach and explain all he had accomplished prior to joining the team. He simply showed everyone what he *could* do—what potential he had. This underdog mindset—having something to prove—served him well. It paid off, too. Much to the chagrin of football fans everywhere, he led his teams to ten Super Bowls, seven of which they won. Not bad for the 199th draft pick.

When I'm sitting across from a candidate I often wonder: *What will this person bring to the company after they learn the company's way of doing business?* When I am recruiting someone, I may be aware that the person is not the most experienced candidate, but if they have a killer attitude and a willingness to prove themselves, I'm confident they will succeed. The reality is that today, people are more likely than ever to be hired based on "potential." Companies often prefer to hire someone without experience who they can put through their own management training. They'd rather not spend time dealing with baggage and bad habits that candidates have learned elsewhere.

So how do you get your edge back? How do you get that killer attitude—after twenty-plus years of working in an industry?

KNOWLEDGE VERSUS LEARNING

At a workforce conference many years ago, Candace listened to the head of a global IT company as they debated with the head of a global consulting company over a question: "What's more important, knowledge or learning?"

"We hire people who are the smartest people in the room," the consultant said. "They know how to do things. They know how to fix things. They know how to build things. They know stuff."

The global IT company head said: "Knowledge is not useful to us because the minute you think you know something, you become invested in making sure it stays true—because then you're the expert. As long as nothing changes, you're still the expert. But in our world, things change every day. So we don't want someone who's invested in the status quo. We want someone who is wide open to learning what's happening next, discovering what's happening next—or creating what's happening next."

That's how you keep the fire burning—by feeling like a beginner and by embracing the beginner's mindset. Business leaders don't necessarily want someone with "all the answers" to come in and "make an impact on" their culture. They want someone who's going to come in and *adapt* to their culture.

I recently met with a former CIO who was very upfront with me. "I could never go back and be a Number Two. From now on, I'm only interested in being Number One." What am I supposed to do with that? He's immediately limiting his choices—and mine—with that mindset. "I'm never going to work for someone who has less credentials and experience than me." Wow.

Most people don't realize that they limit themselves with these high, "limitless" expectations. In a world filled with positive affirmations and "no limits" thinking, I know this is an unpopular opinion. I'm going to be the one to say it: Limitless thinking limits you in your career. This mindset is holding them back because it's focused only on moving up. They don't see the possibilities that exist in moving over or moving on. If they were open to all possibilities, there would be a lot more options out there for them.

In her book *Lean In,* author Sheryl Sandberg argues that the days of joining a corporation and staying there to climb that one ladder are long gone.[2] Pattie Sellers, the former managing editor of *Fortune* magazine and CEO of Sellers Easton Media, conceived of a much better metaphor, stating that "Careers are a jungle gym, not a ladder."[3] A ladder means people can only move up or down, on or off. But in a jungle gym, people have more space for creative exploration. And while there is only one way to get to the top of a ladder, there are many ways to get to the top of a jungle gym.

In some ways, I think "limitless thinking" and expecting only to be "moving up" or in one direction is a way of avoiding what clients are really worried about. If they got brutally honest with themselves, they might realize that deep down they are worried that their best days are behind them. That's why they are always talking about their past accomplishments and glory days. But this too requires a mindset shift. What if you asked yourself: *Couldn't my best days be ahead of me?* Isn't there so much more you could do, learn, and become? If you can be open to listening and figuring out how your past skills plus your personal traits, strengths, and wisdom can serve others, what more could you be capable of doing?

This is the truth about hiring: Companies hire people to solve problems. In fact, they *only* employ people when they have a problem to solve or a gap to fill. So how can you, no matter what your title or role, help solve that problem for them? How can you bridge the gap?

If you stop for a moment and take a deep breath before speaking in interviews, and listen to what problems, challenges, and opportunities the company has at the moment, you're one step closer to being able to answer that question.

THE REFRAME

Once you start to shift your thinking from "my best days are behind me" to "my best days are ahead of me," doors will begin to open for you. The most important step in shifting your mindset is being able to let go of the "I'm so important" syndrome, which looks/sounds like: "My needs are more important than your time" or "You'd be lucky to have me" or "I could do your job" attitude. Shift your mindset instead to "Your time and needs are just as valuable as my own" and "I can help you solve a problem" and "I am willing to learn what I need to do so and work with you to improve my skills." You'll find it will make an enormous difference in how you approach an interview—and how you're perceived.

So this month, we'll be reframing your mindset to become coachable, adaptable, curious, and open to receiving feedback. These are the skillsets that are some of the most critical and foundational to remaining relevant.

BE COACHABLE

I am always ready to learn,
although I do not always like being taught.

—**Winston Churchill**

PRACTICE EXCELLENCE WHERE YOU ARE.

Jennifer worked for the Superintendent of Schools office for twenty-five years. She'd received all the scheduled promotions and benefits, was well liked by everyone in her office, and knew everything about everything. She was, in a word, comfortable. She enjoyed her work and believed she would spend the next fifteen years or so up to retirement in the same position. So imagine her shock and dismay when the new superintendent sat her down during a review and told her she was on probation. She'd most likely be unemployed the following school year if she didn't attend some training and technology classes. Jennifer was floored. At first she was angry and hurt. Didn't this new superintendent know all she had done for the school district in the past? Hadn't her office systems proven effective for twenty-five years? Why change now? She was "only" (in her mind) fifteen years from retirement. Why should she go back to school and take classes again? Why not just coast to retirement, doing things the way they'd always been done?

The superintendent didn't agree. Education was changing and technology was changing at lightning speed. The superintendent wanted to bring the office up to date. There were several inefficiencies that Jennifer could not see because she hadn't experienced any other office in decades. Jennifer's immediate response was to resist this news. "There's nothing wrong with me or how I do things! This new boss is unreasonable! She's ageist! She just wants to replace me with someone younger whom she can pay less."

Now look at it from the superintendent's point of view. She didn't fire Jennifer; she set a clear boundary and gave her some expectations and new goals to shoot for—she was asking Jennifer to be open to learning new things. In other words, to being coachable.

Candace sees people like Jennifer every day in her practice. They come to her feeling stuck and frustrated. They don't see why they are the ones who must change when new bosses or systems are introduced. They also don't aspire to C-suite positions or "limitless" opportunities. They're good at what they do and they never cause trouble. They want to keep their job, their benefits, and retire comfortably. The problem is that this mindset paves the way for complacency.

Candace recommends the idea of *practicing excellence where you are.* That means that, no matter where you are and what you are doing, you ask yourself: What can I improve? My performance? The process? The outcome? What skills and abilities do I need to hone, practice, or brush up on? What recent technologies could I learn? What problems can I set about solving in the office? It means looking at your job as if it were your first day. What would you do differently if this were Day One of your new job?

It's important to remember that not all experience is great experience; you may have worked for many years in a toxic atmosphere or with complacent bosses or peers, and it's possible to absorb those traits, too. Just because you have been employed somewhere for twenty years doesn't necessarily mean all the experiences you have had and the things you've learned are assets. Being open and coachable requires some tough love—that is, tough conversations—and being open to hearing what more is required of you.

There's no doubt this feels scary. As you gain experience and age, the threat of being pushed out by someone younger or with fresher technology skills, and who is willing to work more for less, becomes very real. It's more important than ever to remain vital and relevant to your company's culture. That means being willing to move with changes, maybe even instigating changes of your own. It means offering to take on more responsibility. It means switching up your routine. It means asking: What can I reasonably accomplish today? What else can I do that would be of service?

When we do more than the minimum, or the usual, we feel accomplished. And this feeling of accomplishment flows over into our attitude and into our work. It's energizing, and it's impossible for employers not to see it.

If you're cruising or coasting—waiting for the weekend or for retirement in five, ten, fifteen, or twenty years—you're wasting your time and your employer's. And let me assure you, they can see it and feel it when you bring that attitude and energy to the workplace, too.

One of Candace's heroes, author Seth Godin, offers a course on freelancing through Udemy that made a dramatic difference in her career. He asked, "If you're a freelancer, and you subcontracted your work, would anyone notice? Is your work different or unique enough to be identifiable—and missed?"[1] The reason he asked that was to point out the bigger question: "Are you replaceable?" To be irreplaceable, you have to figure out a way to become so unique, so different, that only you could do the job. No one else could get the same results without your input or guidance.

So I am going to ask you, right now: *In what ways are you replaceable?* What jobs do you do today that anyone (with some training) could do? Another way to look at it is: If you were to get sick and couldn't return to work tomorrow, how likely would it be that the people and the work would move on without you? Most likely they would carry on. In fact, most workplaces do just that every day. We're trained to believe that we're all replaceable.

And it's true. Your team and your company will be able to function without you—that's outside your control. But you can control how hard it is for them to find someone with your unique blend of skills and experience. They can fill the position, but they can't replace *you*. That's what happens when you find a way to be unique and excellent, whatever your role in the company.

So: *In what areas are you unique and excellent?* And if you can't name any, then a little coaching can help you identify or develop them. Start by looking at where the gaps are in your office or on your team—what isn't being done, or done well? What do you hear others routinely complain about? Is this a problem you can solve? If not right now, can you learn the necessary skills required to solve it? Is there a class, a coach, a technology that can help you solve for X? Are you up for taking on something new and mastering it? If you could be The King of X or The Queen of X, what would X be? What would get the attention of your manager or the leadership team? What skill or talent would you be able to take with you to the next phase of your career?

Mini-Exercise: Write down two or three gaps you know frustrate your team or your managers. Then ask:

- Which of these is most important to the company?

- Which of these is most appealing to you, or the best fit for your skills?

- How might you start taking on this challenge or role?

SETTING YOURSELF APART

How do you know you are excellent? When Candace is coaching a group, she will use this as an example of what makes someone excellent: "You will often hear an employer say, 'I just need to hire an accountant.'" It can be *any* accountant. That means they are looking for a commodity. *Any competent worker* will do. Excellence is not really the point. And this level of worker is always replaceable.

But say they're looking for an accountant with a specialized skillset, like a forensic accountant. Employers recognize they're going to have to pay more for that, but they are willing to pay more because this type of accountant requires a different skillset. Hard to replace easily.

But what happens when the employer says "I want the *best* accountant in the city"? What they are saying then is that money is no object. The expectation is that this accountant will be the most skilled accountant on the market, and worth every penny. There's only one "best." Consider them irreplaceable.

But I know that there's even a level above that. When someone calls you by name—that's when you know you have cornered excellence in the market. "Get me Candace Moody on the phone" translates to you being a market of one. You are unique *and* irreplaceable. You are in control. You hold the cards.

And the way to do that is to *practice excellence every day*. It means finding out what you don't know and taking the required courses to be better. It means taking on projects that will push and challenge you but will ultimately give you a competitive edge. It means being committed to improving. It means being motivated to change and striving for the best possible outcomes. It means being coachable.

> "We are what we repeatedly do. Excellence,
> then, is not an act, but a habit."
>
> —**Aristotle**

HOW TO BE COACHABLE

Think of becoming coachable as a version of therapy. First, you admit that there's a problem—and that it might be a "me" problem, rather than a "rest of the world" problem. If you have a long list of reasons why things aren't working out for you, or you hear yourself complaining—a lot—about work, your boss, your team, in fact, everyone else, take a step back and realize that the common denominator in all your problems just might be you.

Once you recognize your role in your current situation, you have to believe that it is fixable. Sitting back, crossing your arms, and taking the defensive stance of "Hey, this is just who I am! Deal with it!" is not helpful. And it's this mindset that will keep you stuck. If you say you're bad at math, tell everyone else you are bad at math, and don't practice math, then you will indeed be bad at math. The same applies elsewhere. How often do you hear someone say, "I am a bad speller"? This is interesting when you think about it. Who among us is born knowing how to spell? No one! It's something we *all had to learn*. We had to study and memorize. And for most of us mortals, we must continue to do so throughout our reading and writing career. (Yes, you can rely on spellcheck, but as we all know, even that lets us down on occasion.) Spelling is one small, universally acknowledged and required skillset. But it's just one of many. We've all heard someone we know announce: "I'm not a people person." Well, not with that attitude! If you want to be a people person, you have to work at getting to know and becoming interested in other people. It takes practice to put yourself out there. Another statement I often hear is: "I don't take orders from others. I have a problem with authority." Who does like being told what to do? In fact, from the time we are born, we resist it! But it's something we all do. What you really want to say is: "I *don't like* to take orders. I *don't like* to spell. I *don't like* math. I *don't like* X."

Mini-Exercise: Make a list of all the things you say you're not good at. Then ask:

- Are there things you say you "don't like" rather than "It's hard for me"?

- Are any of these things you are simply afraid to fail at? "I don't want to mess up, so it's easier for me to say I don't like it, rather than try."

- Which of these things, if improved, could make a difference in your success?

Getting clear about where we need to improve is imperative to the coachable mindset. You can't ask for help or guidance if you don't know where you need it. There is an old saying I love: "If you're consistently the smartest person in the room, you're in the wrong room." Meaning, we are made better when we are surrounded by people who know more than us, who practice their skills and craft, and who push us to improve as well.

A good coach, like a good therapist, is going to push you to see your blind spots. They will shine a light in the corners of where you need to grow and improve, to help you see things differently. As a career coach, Candace helps people think differently about their careers and this helps them approach their careers differently. And a coach will sometimes point to areas where you might be underestimating, not overestimating.

One of my best hires was Clara, a key leader I recruited from a competitor. I saw in her abilities and skills that she didn't see in herself. I had heard people in the community discussing how great she was, and so I watched her interactions with them. She constantly undersold herself, she talked about the things she didn't do well (as noted previously), and she was hampered by the fact that she didn't have a college degree. She was sure that because she didn't have this degree, she could never be more than a mid-level manager. She did not see herself then in the role she has now.

However, I knew people who worked for her, and from them I knew that she would really do amazing things at CSI. So I hired her and set her up with an executive coach, Dr. Angela Love (angelalove.com). Clara's coachability was off the charts. She started with zero confidence that she could do something bigger and ended up leading an organization that has since doubled in size. She's now running the organization like a badass. And it was all possible because she didn't have a chip on her shoulder. She didn't come in as a top-tier executive who wouldn't "take a number two position"; in fact, quite the opposite. She didn't think she could manage in such a high-level position, but she did because she was open to being coached. She *learned* how to become a leader, how to mentor, delegate, and influence. About all of which she had originally said, "That's not me. That's not what I do."

But once she changed her mindset from "I don't think I can" to "I can" and, more importantly, to "I'm willing to give it a shot," that's when doors opened for her. Clara now leads teams and projects all around the country. Just twenty-four months ago, I couldn't get her to introduce a presentation to the leadership team. Thanks to her willingness to learn, to step out of her comfort zone, and to see things differently, she was able to become the leader we'd envisioned.

What made her the ideal coachable person and the success story she is? She didn't believe she was the most experienced or the smartest person in the room. In fact, she knew she wasn't. Clara didn't think she had the most skills or the required education. She wasn't the most senior. She wasn't a man with an MBA. She was simply someone who listened well and was willing to do whatever it took to improve her organization.

Another point I'd like to make—and this is important—is that she *listened* when I gave her feedback. She trusted me and came to believe what I saw. And she was willing to take a risk.

The most important part of the coachable mindset is *believing* that you can change, that you have power to make things better. Even if no one else believes in you right now, I'm giving you permission to be the one person who believes in you. I invite you to become your own coach.

Remember, no matter where you are on your work journey—whether you're still climbing to the top of a mountain, hanging on to a cliff with a death grip, or waiting to be rescued on your way down—you have to believe you can always improve. There are always opportunities to learn, grow, and push yourself.

PRACTICE BEING COACHABLE.

Coachability is like a muscle—it can be strengthened with practice. When we're young, we're usually game to try anything—falling is part of the fun. (If it weren't, babies would never learn to walk.) But as we become older and more self-conscious, we start to avoid things we're not good at. We worry about feeling stupid, looking silly, losing the game, or . . . just falling. So we stop trying new things, especially in our careers. That's why we suggest trying something new that's completely unrelated to your career. When you start learning something new, you can be a beginner again; you expect to do it wrong, to look silly—even to literally fall down. You know you'll need a coach to learn the skill and/or get better. You know that someone out there knows more than you do about this thing, and you're wide open to their advice, to coaching, and correction. Which is the opposite of how you may feel in your career. So, here are a few things to try. Don't be afraid to ask for help and advice; it will strengthen your coachability. And you might have fun as you learn!

1. Find a friend, neighbor, or acquaintance who is a native speaker of another language. Bonus points for choosing a language that's not commonly heard in the U.S. (like Spanish or French). Ask this person to teach you some phrases and to help you read and pronounce them like a native speaker. Commit to practicing, and to being willing to be corrected, over and over until you get it right. (Be sure to include "thank you for your help" as one of your phrases.)

2. Try out a new sport or pastime: golf, skateboarding, ballroom dancing, painting, cooking, juggling, playing an instrument, or pottery. Hire a professional coach to give you a few lessons. (Paying for lessons means you'll get the best coaching they can offer and that you'll also be invested in getting better.) Take notes or video your progress, so you can see the difference between where you started and how you improved with coaching.

3. Ask someone younger than you (it could even be one of your children or grandchildren) to explain how to do something you've never done before. This could be a new dance step, playing a complex board game or video game, or showing you how to do their hobby or a school assignment. Treat them like the expert they are—ask questions about why they do it this way, how they learned what worked best, and why they chose to learn it in the first place. Ask them to teach you how to do it just like they do—and let them critique the results to help you improve.

BE ADAPTABLE

If you change the way you look at things,
the things you look at change.

—Wayne Dyer

J ack was a career journalist. One day he showed up for work only to be told his job no longer existed. "Thank you, Jack. You've done great work, but we're outsourcing from now on." In an instant, Jack was out of a job. And it wasn't as if he had anywhere else to go. The prior two decades, specifically with the dawn of the internet, blogs, twenty-four-hour cable news cycles, and the rise of freelancing (gig work), have decimated newspapers and dailies. Many local newspapers now choose to publish syndicated stories from national news agencies and no longer hire local reporters. Journalists, who have spent years studying their craft and honing their skills on the beat or in newsrooms, have found themselves out of work and out of options.

This was devastating news to Jack and his peers. Being a journalist was all he cared about—it was as much a calling as it was a job. It was incredibly frustrating because Jack knew that it takes an experienced, trained, and empathetic human to be able to talk to people, interpret the news, and report a compelling story. Knowing that his job could so easily be replaced was a hard pill to swallow. *Reporting was all he knew.* Jack was in his fifties and he had a family and a mortgage. He had spent his entire career working toward this position and he was never going to find a job *exactly* like it.

So, Jack went to Candace for career coaching, hoping she could help him find another journalism job. But Candace got him thinking differently. She helped him let go of his identity as a newsroom reporter, and rethink or reframe his career—not in terms of *who*, but of *what*. Instead of thinking of himself as a "reporter" (who), Jack needed to think of the skills (what) he had to offer.

Candace pitched him the idea of freelancing—essentially splitting up his time and sharing his writing and information-gathering skills with multiple clients. Paradoxically, this would provide more job security, not less. If the world was shifting to a gig economy, then Jack needed to shift with it. Otherwise, he needed to consider another career altogether. Candace pointed out, "When you have multiple clients instead of a single employer, it takes several people to fire you, not just one, in order to put you out of work."

Jack was resistant at first. As a freelancer or gig worker, he would be in charge of his own destiny but he'd also . . . *be in charge of his own destiny*. It was a double-edged sword—and it scared him. If he wasn't out finding clients, constantly networking, or generating his own income or opportunities, he'd be out of work all over again. Only this time he'd be firing himself. There was a lot of risk involved.

Jack didn't want to incur all that risk. But Candace essentially asked him, "What do you have to lose? You're in a bind. You need to make money. Why not give it a try?"

Jack acquiesced, but with the caveat, "I'm going to charge something outrageous. And, I'll prove to you, Candace, that freelancing can't replace my work."

To his surprise, his first client accepted his offer. Jack had been averaging a little over thirty dollars an hour as a staff reporter (based on all the hours he put in); now he was able to charge a hundred dollars an hour to write.

Jack's story has a happy ending because he was willing to make himself relevant and to keep up with the changes in his industry. Like so many employees, Jack took his job for granted and believed that it would always be there. He thought he was "safe." But the truth was that he was never safe. The world shifted under him overnight. And it can happen to anyone, at any time. As long as you're working for someone else, you'll never have 100 percent control over your destiny. But there are things you can do—whether as a full-time employee or a gig worker—to set up some guardrails. The best guardrail is your mindset—particularly, your ability to adapt to whatever situation arises.

"Change before you have to."

–Jack Welch

ADAPTABILITY IS NOT A REACTION, IT'S A SKILL.

Adaptability is something you need to work on before a crisis comes to you. It's based on the realization that no one is safe and things can change at any minute. It's also the ability to adjust to these changes, which means always thinking ahead and asking yourself some tough questions.

Several years ago, Brian came into my office. He was a civil engineer who was deeply unsatisfied with his career. He'd come to realize that every year, he would work hard, receive a small bonus, and maybe make

5 to 10 percent more each year until he retired. Raises would cover his cost-of-living increases, but he would be working hard for essentially the same amount of money for the rest of his life. Like so many who come to me, Brian wondered what more he could be doing: *What more am I capable of? Is this all there is?* At the same time, he saw people who were in sales, earning commissions, and they seemed to be more in control of their destiny. After talking, I suggested he explore sales as a career option. Brian was smart and credentialed. He was a good-looking guy, an excellent communicator, and he thought quickly on his feet. Eventually, he accepted a sales position at a machinery company, where his engineering background made him very valuable, and is now incredibly successful. His income is now only limited by his energy and commitment, which he has in abundance.

What I love about Brian's story is he took the bull by the horns. He spent some time assessing where he was at and where he was going, and when he didn't like the outcome, he adapted and made a change. How many people have the courage to ask themselves what Brian did: "If I stay on the path I am on now and fast-forward my life ten years, will I like where I end up?" If the answer is no, then it's time to make some changes. Instead of reacting to a crisis, Brian anticipated one and adapted ahead of time.

Now, many people might say, "What crisis? He had a safe and dependable income." But the crisis for Brian would have been a future life he was deeply unsatisfied with and a job he resented. If he stayed on that path, there would have been a crisis eventually—maybe when he no longer had the energy to forge a new path. Fortunately, he anticipated his own outcomes. He weighed the risk of staying in the same career or making a leap and pushing himself. Sometimes being adaptable is about assessing the path you are currently on and measuring it against the opportunities and risks of a different path.

THE KEY TO ADAPTABILITY: ASSESSING
WHAT IS IN YOUR CONTROL AND WHAT ISN'T

Both Jack's and Brian's stories represent two ways change can present itself and how it requires you to respond and adapt differently. At work, there will be many situations in which you have no control. There will be economic downturns, a change in leadership or company ownership, a sudden demotion, or an assignment that stretches your capacity. These are the times that usually take you by surprise, and when you feel powerless to change the circumstances. All you can change is your reaction. In Jack's case, he was forced to react to a situation; in Brian's case, he anticipated the situation (a future mid-career crisis as a civil engineer) and pivoted, switching his career to sales. Both men faced the moment by assessing what was in and outside of their control and then adapting accordingly.

Sometimes being adaptable means recognizing whether you have a *problem* or a *situation*. As Seth Godin says, problems have solutions whereas situations do not. A problem may require some form of sacrifice or trade off to reach its solution, but "Situations are simply things we need to live with." We can only begin to move on when we accept that a problem we have is really a situation. "Focusing on a situation is usually a source of stress, not a way forward."[1]

One definition of adaptability is learning to thrive within a situation, rather than trying to fix it. Being adaptable does not make you automatically comfortable with change. It's hard to change—in fact, we all resist it on some level. But change is the one constant in life. You can't fix that, but you can become more adept at being adaptable.

The first step is to become aware of the change and your reaction to it. What part of the new situation bothers you? Why are you stressed? You might be surprised at the answers after you sit with these questions for a while. You may find that once you name some of your emotions (envy, disappointment, anger), they have less power over you. Emotions are weather; your personality is the climate. You can wait out some bad weather.

The second step is to get comfortable with being uncomfortable. The world is constantly changing, so trying to stay comfortable is a fruitless endeavor. Just when you get comfortable, chances are you will need to change again. Recognizing discomfort without trying to kill it, get stressed about it, or hide it from yourself is bringing you one step closer to managing it—and possibly letting it go.

There will be many situations in which you will be called to adapt—to a new boss, a new process, new personality on the team, a new assignment. Simply ask yourself: *What is in my control? What isn't?*

Mini-Exercise: Imagine yourself in the following scenarios. Then ask: What is in my control and what is not?

- Your company has just been sold and is under new ownership. There are rumors that there might be layoffs and restructuring.

- You are assigned a new manager, but she is different from your previous leader; she requires many more tasks than you are used to. You feel micromanaged and overworked.

- Your company has downsized and you have been assigned a new position. You lost your office and must now work shoulder-to-shoulder with employees you previously led.

- You've been working from home for three years, but now your company is requiring you to come back to the office.

At first glance, all of these scenarios are outside of your control. You can't control whether your company is bought or sold. You can't choose a new manager or boss. You don't have a lot of flexibility, especially if you're a full-time employee, to tell your boss that you don't want to change roles. And many people, who have been faced with similar situations while working from home, don't have a lot of choice in returning to the office or not. While you may not have a lot of control over these situations, you still have choices. You can adjust your mindset to make the changes more tolerable, if not more advantageous to you in the long run.

For example, if there are changes afoot in your organization, what can you do to make sure your leaders know you're willing to shift with those changes? Or, if you have heard that there are going to be layoffs, it might be time to start brushing up your resume and checking in with old contacts. In other words: prepare. If you have been assigned a new manager, what can you do to mitigate any misunderstandings? Can you meet with them to frankly address your concerns and/or working styles to figure out the best way to make the relationship work? If you have been assigned a new role that you didn't ask for or want, how can you make it better for yourself on a daily basis? What small things can you do to make your new workstation feel more like your own? Is there anyone on your new team willing to go out for lunch or happy hour? Are there new connections and friendships to be made? If you work from home and are asked to return to the office, are there terms you can negotiate? Is there flexibility to structure your day differently? How can you reframe the situation? In other words, how can you look at it differently and start taking charge of the things that are actually within your control?

YOU HAVE MORE CONTROL THAN YOU THINK.

After you have assessed the situation and considered what you have control over, one of the most effective ways to adapt to it is by reframing the story you tell yourself. When things happen that are out of our control, we can feel powerless or worse, like a failure. Adam Grant, an organizational psychologist and best-selling author of books like *Option B* and *Think Again*, argues that the ability to adapt and change comes out of resilience. To adapt to various situations, it's helpful to assess every challenge and to remember the "Three Ps"—that whatever is happening isn't Personal, Permanent, or Pervasive. What that means is that if you are dealing with a problem at work, it's not usually about you as a person; it might be about an aspect of your job, but it's not about you. It's not permanent (remember everything can and will change, even this situation, eventually). And it's not pervasive (i.e., if you are falling short in one area of life, it doesn't mean you're falling short in every area).[2] Simply reframing the situation can shift your entire mindset, taking you from feeling "powerless to change" to "empowered to change." Some ways to do that include reframing your identity, rethinking your vision, and even updating how people perceive you.

Paul had formerly been a CFO. However, as the world changed, he found himself in a new company as part of an accounting team—as the staff accountant, rather than as the leader of the team. In many ways, it was his own choice. He had climbed the ladder, but at this point in his career he no longer wanted all the stress that came from being in charge. At first, Paul pushed back on his accounting manager's requests, and, as time went on, he was becoming known as a difficult and almost argumentative employee. One of his fellow accountants mentioned that he needed to argue less and just do the work. That valuable piece of feedback turned out to be the catalyst that completely changed Paul's attitude and thus his acceptance by the team. Shortly thereafter, he embraced his task-oriented job and enjoyed not worrying about always being right or making decisions. The last time I spoke to him, he was happily employed and loving his new arrangement. Simply by resetting his career goals and adjusting his identity from "boss" to "team member," he was able to adapt.

Several people I've placed over the years felt like they failed when they took a "lesser" role. Often, having a frank conversation with your new supervisor or director can help reset your career goals. When you've been the person in charge and enjoyed some of the perks that go with a big title, it may feel like you've somehow failed by reporting to someone else, someone who may even be younger than you. Being adaptable means accepting this new reality and figuring out how to grow from there.

One of my favorite examples is of a local professional, Josh, who was a senior lending officer with a big-name bank. He wined and dined clients, went to fun lunches and events, and played a lot of golf. However, when the economy changed after the financial crisis, Josh was forced to switch banks and went back into a production role. At first, he was miserable and seriously considered switching careers. Instead, he spoke to one of his directors who, Josh recounted, "resold me on the dream." Josh's boss reminded him that the economy ebbs and flows and that things would come back. He was encouraged to stay the course. As it turns out, a lot of his new peers did leave, but Josh worked through the downturn. When the banking crisis was over, his new company rewarded his work and loyalty. He is still employed with the company and manages all their local correspondent lending.

Years ago, we hired Pam, a former executive, and placed her in a lesser management role than she was used to, one that required her to oversee many of our administrative staff. Instead of sitting in an office, she sat out on the floor with them. At first, no one invited her to anything and she felt very isolated. She wasn't part of the executive team, and she didn't feel accepted by the team she managed. After some time, she realized that while she was complaining about not fitting in, she wasn't trying to figure out *how* to fit in. So, she started catching up on interests relevant to her team—the TV shows they watched, the concerts they attended, and the restaurants they liked. She decided to get out of her comfort zone and invite her team to events she knew they'd like. One day, she invited several teammates to a local outdoor concert where they saw Iggy Azalea perform. Although she had no idea who Iggy was, her team was thrilled. Those who joined the event quickly changed their opinion of her, and Pam went on to develop a great rapport with her team.

If Pam hadn't stopped and wondered how she could change, she never would have. It wasn't a radical change, either. She simply had to think deeply about the situation, assess what she needed to do, and then do it. Most of us have all the tools we need; we just need to know how to use them and have the courage to pick them up.

PIVOTING: ASSESSING AND TRANSFERRING YOUR SKILLS

What Paul, Josh, and Pam did was pivot. They were all skilled individuals who found ways to transfer those skills into new roles. Of course, there is no more iconic image of "pivoting" than the *Friends* TV episode when Ross yells "PIVOT! PIVOT" at Chandler and Rachel while trying to push an unwieldy couch up an apartment building staircase. Making a career shift, or even mindset shift, can feel as uncomfortable (and unlikely) as getting an oversized couch around a tight corner. But unlike moving a couch, a career pivot takes more brains than brawn.

Pivoting is simply taking skills you already have and applying them in a different way. Military personnel have to "pivot" all the time, especially when they retire and move into civilian life. In the military, personnel are usually assigned a job, trained to do that job, and then spend their military career specializing in that job. In a military command, everyone understands their orders: what to do, where to go, and how to measure success. And they do it all exceptionally well. After twenty years of service, experience, and honed expertise, they have earned titles and recognition within a very hierarchical system. Career service members are eligible to retire in their early to mid-forties, which means they still have twenty more years or so of work in front of them.

But even if they've been planning a second career for years, the civilian workforce can feel alien. They may find themselves having to start from scratch in a world where everything is negotiable. While they may have been adept at giving or taking orders in the military, in the civilian world, not everyone wants or feels obligated to follow such orders. In some companies, the organization chart is flat; collaboration is valued as much as—sometimes more than—the leadership skills military veterans have spent years developing. It can feel chaotic, discouraging, and overwhelming.

I know several recruiters who have had difficulty placing military officers in civilian jobs. It's not because the military officers aren't qualified; it's that their skills aren't aligned with the corporate culture they're experiencing for the first time.

Conversely, I've seen former entrepreneurs who want to re-enter the workforce and have had difficulty returning to a structured environment and working under a manager again. They were used to making their own schedules, calling the shots, and working at their own pace. Whether you're moving from a structured environment to a dynamic and ambiguous one, or vice versa, the key is to adapt your skills and your style if you're going to succeed in a new environment. Oprah Winfrey is commonly attributed as having said, "The greatest discovery of all time is that a person can change his future by merely changing his attitude."

STEP ONE TO ADAPTABILITY

The word *adaptation* comes from the Latin *adaptō*, meaning "I fit" or "I adjust to." Biologists define adaptation as the process of adjusting behavior, physiology, or structure to become more suited to an environment. For example, animals learn to survive in new environments by applying their skills in new ways. We humans can also adapt the skills we have to succeed in a new or changing environment. In fact, figuring out which skills to apply in new situations is the very definition of adaptability in the workplace and it's essential to remaining relevant.

Knowing that you have the skills to change when things change around you will give you confidence. You'll know that you can not only survive, but thrive, even when things feel chaotic. People who can't adapt get left behind; teams need to move fast and they can't wait for everyone to adjust and decide they're on board with what's changing right now. Being adaptable means embracing the "lead, follow, or get out of the way" philosophy.

Step one to becoming adaptable is to take a skills inventory. Take a few moments to list the skills you have to offer and that would be useful in your current or ideal role. (Remember, not all your skills will be listed on your resume.) The best way to adapt is to transfer the skills you already have into a new job. Soft or personal skills are those that deal with communication, interpersonal interactions, critical-thinking, or leadership. Hard skills are typically job-specific and technical. Not all hard skills will be transferable to every job, but many soft skills will be.

Hard/Technical Skills

These skills include your education, training, and certifications. They also include the work you've done over the course of your career. For example, if you're in Finance, you may have enterprise system proficiency or accounting system experience.

Exercise: Skills Inventory

Ask yourself what skills you currently possess. Then determine your level of expertise. Is this a skill you enjoy and can see yourself using over the next five to ten years? Or is it a skill you do well, but don't enjoy? Depending on your answer, this may be part of the reason you feel stuck in your job. How could you change your approach or your role to do more or less of this function?

Is there is a skill that you would be interested in developing? Write this down as one or more of the skills you could develop. Then ask yourself, is this a skill that fulfills a need in your company, a trend in the industry or job market, or is it one you would enjoy and that could help you become unique or irreplaceable?

In the space below, list your skills, level of experience, level of enjoyment, and areas in which you would like to be more skilled.

Skill	Level of Expertise	Level of Enjoyment	Want to Become More Skilled

Exercise: Transferable Skills

Transferable skills are skills that can apply to any job or industry. For example, every company needs people with management skills, sales experience, customer service, IT and network management, marketing, human resources, administrative, and accounting skills—you get the idea. When you master one of these core business functions, you can take them with you to almost any company in any industry, which allows you to become productive with very little training.

Transferable skills also provide an opportunity for you to make a career pivot. If you've been in a technical role, you may choose to ramp up or prioritize another skill that improves your marketability, your earnings potential, or your job satisfaction. A pivot to training, sales, project management, or any number of other options will allow you to adapt to new market opportunities while still retaining the value of your technical skills. (Refer back to my story about Brian, the engineer who went into sales.)

In the space below, list your areas of:

Transferable Skills	Expertise	Enjoyment	Needed Improvement/ Skills

Exercise: Personal Skills

You also have personality attributes that employers will value. It's easy for most of us to overlook these traits because many of them come naturally, without training or years of practice. Can't everyone spot a single typo in a complex document at one glance? Isn't everyone a natural at taking things apart and figuring out how they work? Who doesn't enjoy presenting in front of crowds?

Think about skills you have that set you apart from your peers. Make a list and imagine how you'd use the skills to advance your performance, making your work unique and irreplaceable.

Here are some examples to prompt your own inventory, in no particular order:

- Patience/ability to focus/attention to detail
- Outgoing/confident/competitive
- Coachable/adaptable/a change agent
- Creative/innovative/think differently
- Mechanical/technical/investigative skills
- Experience in foreign cultures/multi-lingual/open to new experiences
- Energetic/multi-tasker/driven to succeed
- Empathetic/easily connects to others/great at building meaningful relationships

What do you bring to the table that makes you unique? How is your approach to work special and different from those of your peers? How did you develop these skills or traits? How will they benefit your employer? How will they benefit you in adapting to new challenges, new opportunities, or a new role? In the space below, list your personal skills:

Personal Skills

Exercise: Assess your current situation.

If you feel stuck, uncertain, or threatened by your current situation, then this exercise will help you analyze what is happening and determine what action might be useful, if any.

What is the situation? In a few sentences, describe what's happening right now and how you feel about it.

Here are some examples:

> *I have not been able to get a job and I'm panicking about being able to survive financially.*
>
> *I just got passed over for my third promotion. I'm afraid I have hit a wall at my company.*
>
> *My new boss doesn't appreciate my work. I'm worried that they're looking for a reason to fire me.*
>
> *I'm not included in high-level meetings anymore and I'm beginning to feel pushed out.*
>
> *I hate my job, but I have no idea how to find a better one—I don't even know what I want to do.*

Your situation:

_____

_____

_____

_____

Is the situation (Circle the answer that applies):

- ○ Personal? Yes / No/ I'm not sure

- ○ Pervasive? Yes / No/ I'm not sure

- ○ Permanent? Yes / No/ I'm not sure

In a few sentences, describe:

_____

_____

_____

_____

What factors in the situation are out of your control?

What factors are in your control?

What feels like the safest option(s) for you right now? Why?

What feels like the riskiest option(s) for you right now? Why?

What would be the best outcome if you took the risk on any of the options above?

What would be the worst outcome if you took the risk on any of the options above?

What might be the outcome if you took no action? Can you live with that?

Reframe the situation so that it is more in your control. What does that look like?

Reframe the situation so that it's less of a threat and more of an opportunity. What changed?

What could you change that would make the situation more bearable or less scary?

What step could you take right now toward making the situation better?

PRO-TIP: ADAPTING IN THE AGE OF FLEXIBLE WORKSPACES

One of the reasons that CSI thrived during COVID was that we became excellent at hosting Zoom happy hours. It was a huge hit and our clients loved it. Everyone was desperate for social connection, so we stepped in and filled in the void. Instead of opting out, we used the opportunity to find a new and different way to connect with our clients and our employees. Of course, CSI wasn't alone in having to change the way we did business; everyone had to pivot during COVID. Within days, companies had to change their entire workforce model, shutting down on a Friday and becoming completely remote by Monday. Technology played a huge role and our employees rolled with the changes, using Zoom, Slack, Teams, Google, you name it. Employees all over the world quickly adapted to the "new normal."

Now employers are demanding that employees return to the office and these employees are resisting. They've already "changed" in their minds. And going back to the office has real-life consequences.

Other employers found that remote workers were highly productive; they were able to cut overhead costs and don't want to switch back. Whether the company you work for has decided to go fully remote, has adopted a hybrid model, or requires you to return to the office—you'll need to adjust accordingly or consider switching positions, companies, or careers to find a model that suits your skills and needs. During the pandemic, we had no choice in the matter; we had to adapt or we'd be out of business or out of work.

This is where you need to take some personal responsibility and assess your own skills, personality, and willingness to adapt. I know some people who were workaholics during the pandemic; they didn't know when to shut the laptop. Without a finite end to the day, they kept going . . . and going . . . and going. But I also know people who couldn't survive without structure or social interaction.

Work from Home

After speaking to many of our employees, as well as employees from other companies about their success or failures, here are a few of the successful WFH strategies:

1. Establish a routine.

2. Treat the situation as if you were still going into an office. Go through your normal pre-work routine—set your alarm, shower, work out (if you do that), eat your breakfast, dress for the workday.

3. Establish an actual office in your residence or create one somewhere where you can get away from distractions.

4. Become an expert at protecting your time. Don't let Zoom calls and requests at work prevent needed breaks in your day. Schedule time to exercise, breaks to unplug, and end at a reasonable stop in your day.

5. Establish clear expectations from supervisor(s). Many of the people I've spoken with found that they were getting work requests well into the evening and on weekends. Set up an out-of-office email response for outside-of-office working hours.

6. Request regular feedback from your supervisor(s) on the quantity and quality of your work. Now that you're not seeing each other daily, it's important to make sure you're aligned on how much you're getting accomplished each day.

One of my favorite tips comes from an employee, Erin, who successfully transitioned to full-time remote work. She said, "I learned that I had to put my shoes on or I never felt like I was at work." Erin found that to be successful, she had to set up an office and commit to only working while in that office. Otherwise she says would have felt the need to work even while cooking dinner.

Hybrid

Many companies continue to offer a hybrid work environment, where employees can choose to work two or three days in the office and then work two or three days from home. Our polling suggests that the flexibility is based on maintaining certain productivity standards. Some of the suggestions for a successful hybrid work arrangement include:

1. Clarify expectations for this new arrangement. Work out with your supervisor(s) exactly what hybrid will look like, including how often to check in and the completion of tasks.

2. Maintain a routine. Some people find that hybrid work feels like they are constantly in flux. However, consistently working from home the same days each week can help. Establish a routine that helps impose some consistency. Get up at the same time each day, get ready, and go to your favorite coffee shop. Then either go into the office or to your home office to start your day.

Return to Office

There are competing trends in the workplace with many companies becoming more flexible with work from home, while others are bringing their workforce back into the office. If you find yourself in this situation, the following scenarios may help:

1. Ask if you can try hybrid first before going back to the office. For example, if you've been working from home since COVID, and your company is now requiring you to come into the office, ask them to work with you on a transition plan. We find that many clients are willing to do this even if it's for a brief period. It may help you begin re-establishing an office routine.

2. Immerse yourself in the corporate culture. For many people, making the best of the situation was how they adapted to their new reality. This could mean re-engaging with your coworkers by going out to lunch together or attending a company happy hour.

3. Develop new relationships. Many people successfully and happily jumped back into their office routine by finding people who could relate to the challenges they faced with the return to the office. Use these new relationships to help you embrace the situation and find the silver lining in it.

The Bottom Line

You must be honest about what you're doing and how you can best contribute to your workplace. Ask yourself: Why are you truly resistant to returning to the office? Are you worried your productivity will slip? That you do your best work when you're on your own?

Understanding why you feel the way you do will help you align to your work style. Once you understand your work style you can work and adapt anywhere! For example, if you are a self-starter and you don't need to be in the office to be productive—then you will be productive in any office. If you're someone who is task orientated, knows what needs to get done, and does it, theoretically you would thrive anywhere—office or remote.

I have an employee who, long after the office has closed, is still working. When I received an email at three in the morning, I realized that this was a person who needed to be told to slow down or stop. Whether she is here in the office or at home, she is constantly "on." People like her are amazing for an institution, but they can quickly burn out if not reined in. On the other side of the spectrum is the person who struggles with self-motivation, procrastination, or a lack of structure or ambiguity. When working remotely, they are going to need some adaptive strategies to help stay on task. That might look like building out a calendar with set tasks during the day, scheduling meetings at optimal times that don't interrupt the workflow. It may mean setting up a system with a manager for daily check-ins and task reporting (or using a workflow app to do so).

Regardless of where you're working, you need to find strategies that work for you—it begins with the mindset—a willingness to adapt, but to also be curious about your capabilities, strengths, and talents, as well as others you work with and for.

WEEK 3

GET CURIOUS

Be curious, not judgmental.

— **Walt Whitman**

BE CURIOUS, NOT JUDGMENTAL.

One of my favorite TV shows is *Ted Lasso*. Ted is an American football coach who suddenly finds himself coaching soccer in England. He's not even sure why an English soccer team has taken a risk by hiring him. Unbeknownst to him, his boss, Rebecca, only hired Ted because she expects him to fail. She hopes that Ted will ruin her ex-husband's beloved soccer team. Though he doesn't understand why he's been hired, Ted clearly knows that everyone underestimates him. During a pivotal scene in a bar, Rebecca's ex-husband taunts Ted; he bets him that he can't even win a game of darts. Ted accepts the wager. He stands up in front of everyone and says, "Guys have underestimated me my entire life and for years I never understood why—it used to really bother me. Then one day I was driving my little boy to school, and I saw a quote by Walt Whitman. It was painted on the wall and it said, 'Be curious, not judgmental.' I like that." As Ted finishes his monologue, he throws the dart and lands a bullseye, winning the bet.[1] In that one scene, the entire premise of Ted Lasso is revealed: *Be Curious, Not Judgmental!* Instead of writing Ted off, he suggests people should get to know him instead. As the show progresses, that is exactly what happens. Ted even learns to not judge himself too harshly. And we the audience get to know not only him, but all his coworkers and team members. A clear throughline is that many of the characters on the show are misunderstood, not just Ted. In the end, we learn that it is better to get to know others a bit more, rather than jumping quickly to conclusions. Curiosity allows for this: By asking questions and looking beyond the surface, we can move past quick (and often inaccurate) judgments.

> "Let go of certainty. The opposite isn't uncertainty.
> It's openness, curiosity and a willingness to embrace
> paradox, rather than choose up sides. The ultimate
> challenge is to accept ourselves exactly as we are,
> but never stop trying to learn and grow."
>
> — **Tony Schwartz**, journalist and business writer

WHAT IF THAT WEREN'T TRUE?

Candace once had a coaching client, Sue, who received a job offer from her organization that was a terrible fit and she was extremely upset about it. "As an introvert, she didn't think she would be cut out for a career in sales. She was insulted that her organization thought she would be good at something she had already clearly expressed she would never be good at," Candace explained.

In response, Candace employed a classic coaching technique. She asked Sue, "What if that weren't true? What if being an introvert didn't make you a bad salesperson? What if it were an advantage instead of a disadvantage?"

As it turned out, the sales job wasn't a typical sales job—it was technical sales. So guess who Sue would sell to? Other introverts! Most technical-minded people don't prioritize lunches or glad-handing. They appreciate people who skip the small talk, do their homework, pay attention to the details, and focus on the facts. Once Sue started to get curious about the sales position, and the advantages for someone like her in a technical sales job, the more interested she became in the position.

Sue's first reaction, to reject the job and get angry, is typical. It's a protective reaction. Trying out new ideas or concepts feels scary, even risky. Being open and curious required Sue to step out of her comfort zone and to be vulnerable. However, this uncomfortable, vulnerable feeling usually passes with time. And getting past this feeling of discomfort is the only way to truly grow.

So how can we move past feelings of resistance or anger? Candace says the best way is to start with that question that confronts your current perceived reality: "What if it weren't true?" This question invites us to get curious about our preconceived notions, unconscious beliefs about ourselves and others of which we may not even be aware. You may have heard things such as:

She's a girly-girl so she's probably not interested in work that gets her hands dirty.

I'm fifty-six years old, so I'll always struggle with new software and these (stupid) messaging apps.

The way I learned is the best way; this kid won't be able to teach me anything I don't know.

He's twenty years older than me. He won't be interested in anything I have to say.

They're from a younger generation; they don't work as hard as we do.

By asking "What if that weren't true?" we invite curiosity where there once was judgment. Building the habit of questioning our first (protective) response opens the door to becoming more curious.

WHAT IF I DID IT A DIFFERENT WAY?

Another way to approach discomfort is to ask, "What if I did it a different way?" If you find yourself doing something over and over and getting the same result, it's time to think about trying something new. (A common definition of insanity is doing something over and over expecting different results.) How often do you stop and look critically at your behaviors and actions? Are you trying the same thing over and over? Do you approach every job interview the same way and wonder when you aren't hired? And do you attribute the problem to someone else, some outside force, every time? Who or what is the common denominator in each situation and what variable can you change? The variables typically are your own behavior and actions. And chances are you may need to try something completely different.

"You need to use your imagination," Candace advises. It takes imagination and curiosity to move from a fixed mindset to one that is growth-oriented. Candace tells her coaching clients to push past the borders of what they can imagine—to see what possibilities show up when they start sentences with "I think I might be able to . . ." or "Wouldn't it be nice if I worked in (insert ideal scenario)." Rather than habitually responding from a protective point of view, pause and try to imagine an alternate reality.

WHAT AN INTERESTING THOUGHT!

Ten years ago, I worked with a corporate manager, Meghan, who was extremely unhappy in her work. Not only was she unsatisfied with the daily grind, but she also lacked direction and purpose.

I asked her, "How would you feel about running a nonprofit? One that aligned with your values and gave you a sense of purpose and meaning?"

From what I could tell, she was extremely skilled at interacting with people and managing budgets. These were transferable skills. Instead of being negative, she became immediately curious.

"Hmm. I've never thought about nonprofit. *That's an interesting thought!*"

With that one statement, *That's an interesting thought*, Meghan invited herself to think more openly about this new career. Instead of *resistance* she met the idea with *interest*.

Immediately, she started asking questions. "So, Chris, why do you think I'd be a good fit? All I have ever known is corporate work. Do you think I am prepared? In what ways could I add value to the organization?"

I explained that a couple of my nonprofit clients were looking for executive directors and that they were looking for someone with precisely her skillsets; they needed someone to manage budgets, fundraise, and engage with people.

"You can do all those things," I explained.

"I *can* do all those things!" she repeated.

Before we met, Meghan thought that because she had only worked in corporate, that's all she could do for the rest of career. But by being curious and looking at her career opportunities through a different lens, she could imagine new possibilities. Three months later, we placed her in a role as the director of a nonprofit. Since then, she has become an executive director for another large nonprofit. It turned out to be an incredible career for her. Instead of being furious, defensive, or protective at a different possibility, Meghan chose to be curious instead.

For some, this is easier said than done. One might argue that Meghan had a naturally positive disposition and was open to new opportunities, something that doesn't come easy to everyone. In fact, I've known plenty of people who are quite the opposite; they seem to be wired for the worst-case scenario. In this case, a kind of Jedi Mind Trick can help them move past it. It's as simple as asking another question . . .

WHAT'S THE WORST THAT COULD HAPPEN?

A common practice in behavioral therapy when dealing with particularly anxious people is to ask them: "So what is the worst thing you think could happen?" By asking someone to dig deeper, they realize that what they fear the most will likely never happen. When it comes to jobs and careers, many people don't try new opportunities because of their fears and fixed beliefs. These people don't realize that the fears that are holding them back—aren't even real. Or if they are real, they're not *deadly*. They will survive.

For example, one of the worst things that could happen in business is some kind of failure. A person might fail at managing other people, creating spreadsheets, or closing deals. They might make a fool of themselves. Another example is the fear of rejection. I can't tell you how often clients say: "What if they don't like me? What if they don't hire me?" The reality is everyone messes up. Everyone fails. However, rarely are mistakes so overwhelming that you can't recover or learn from them. And so what if they reject you? Will you be able to keep looking for new work? Of course. Sometimes the things you're afraid of don't ever happen. But acknowledging and then addressing your fears allows you to imagine possible solutions to even the biggest challenges. And through this practice of acknowledging your fears, you might discover there aren't many challenges you can't overcome. As the old saying goes, you've already survived 100 percent of your worst days. So what makes you think you can't survive one more bad day or an overwhelming obstacle? The only thing stopping you is you.

WHAT IF I GAVE IT A SECOND SHOT?

One reason why you might resist trying something different or new is that you have a "story" around why it isn't for you. Perhaps you tried something years ago and hated it, so have sworn it off forever. Or maybe you didn't have the right skills or education, so you gave up—never testing your own mettle. I remember during the second semester of my freshman year of college, I had to take Principles of Accounting and I hated it. In fact, I despised it so much I decided there was no way I could be a business major. I dropped the class and my major. Now I have to laugh. As the CEO of a company, I am constantly looking at spreadsheets and budgets. Accounting is a critical part of my job.

But when I was a freshman in college, I wasn't ready for it. It was the timing. As the years went by, and as I was exposed to spreadsheets, budgets, and accounting, I became more proficient. Thank goodness I didn't let the story of my life be "I was no good at accounting in college, therefore I can't be a CEO."

Candace's husband has a similar story. He is a medical massage therapist, and he has taught massage therapy for many years. However, he failed Anatomy and Physiology his freshman year of college. Unfortunately, he had a terrible teacher who was incapable of teaching beyond the abstract principles. Once Candace's husband began work in massage therapy and knew healing others was going to be his life's work, anatomy and physiology took on new meaning. It was no longer an abstract concept, but something concrete and relevant to what he was doing as a career. With the time right and a newfound passion, he dove headfirst into learning as much as he could. This was now his craft, not just a test he had to pass. This time around, it was much easier for him to learn anatomy and physiology. He became a teacher, a good one, because he understood how to teach these concepts to people who were a lot like him when he was a freshman in college.

Moral of the story? Just because you tried something once and it didn't work out, doesn't mean you shouldn't try it again. Sometimes it's the timing, sometimes it's the wrong teacher, sometimes you're not in the right place, and sometimes it's the technology that changes.

When Candace was in her MBA program, she believed she wasn't "good at math." She told herself the story, "I'm a words person!" Then a professor showed her a software program that helped her do the math by setting up the problem correctly. Candace was beside herself. "Oh my God, the heavens rained down with joy and glory, because I knew how to set up a killer word problem!"

Sometimes it's truly not about working harder, but smarter. And that can be as simple as shifting your energy and focus. You can spend all your time making a list of why things won't work. Or you could make a list of why things *might work out,* as well as some possibilities that could help you.

Most of us have already learned to pivot a time or two. We have all become resourceful because we've had to. Chances are you are working right now in a job or career you didn't go to college for. According to ResumeBuilder.com, a website that offers resume building support and career advice, less than 50 percent of all those who hold a bachelor's degree work full-time within a field of study related to their major. There are many reasons for this—among them job availability at the time of graduation—but sometimes people just change their minds. And just because something appealed to you (or didn't) at age eighteen, nineteen, twenty, or twenty-one, doesn't mean it will continue throughout your career. The key is to constantly ask yourself the right questions and to be curious about what you're capable of—now and in the future.

> "In the end you don't so much find yourself as you
> find someone who knows who you are."

> —**Robert Brault,** journalist and author

WHO AM I WILLING TO ACCEPT HELP FROM?

As a by-product of becoming more curious, you may become humbler. Or vice versa—the humbler you are, the more curious you become. When this happens, you may need some help. Many people come to me and to Candace because they have exhausted all the possibilities on their own (or at least they think they have).

Once you become curious rather than judgmental, you become more open to asking for help and guidance. Ted Lasso, for example, turns a corner when he enlists the help of a therapist to identify some of his limiting issues. He becomes a better soccer coach when he begins to learn the game by reading, and getting curious, about the differences between American and European football.

It's very hard to reach out to someone and ask for their opinion and guidance. There is always a chance that what they have to say may be at odds with what you believe to be true or the ideas you hold about yourself. They may even suggest changes or observations about your behavior that may be tough to swallow.

Listening to someone else's perception of you, or advice about what you should change, requires you to be humble enough to say the four toughest words in the English Language: "You might be right."

> "The greatest problem with communication is we don't listen to understand. We listen to reply. When we listen with curiosity, we don't listen with the intent to reply. We listen for what's behind the words."
>
> —**Roy T. Bennett,** *The Light in the Heart*

YOU MIGHT BE RIGHT; LET'S TRY IT YOUR WAY.

Over the years, countless people have sat across from me repeating a litany of reasons why they are perfect for a job (including my own). They are loath to admit that they may need some improving, or that they should reconsider certain markets or positions. I know someone is going to be okay, and that we're going to make progress in their job search, when they say, "You might be right" or "Let's try it your way." They finally recognize that the way they viewed job opportunities or presented themselves in job interviews wasn't working, and they are ready to try something new. They are finally in a space where they can listen and really hear what needs to be said. It's as if I could see the veil lift from their eyes—they were ready, truly ready, to make a change. When that happens, I don't see a defensive person sitting before me; I see a curious person.

When people stop complaining, arguing for their current circumstances, or blaming or judging others, they can truly begin to hear what is being said. I can provide all the feedback in the world and offer countless suggestions for change and growth, but until someone is willing to listen—and by that I mean, understand what I am saying and not just prepare a response while I am talking—they will never truly change or grow. As soon as I hear someone say, "Tell me more about that," I know they are ready. They can handle whatever feedback I give them. Getting curious is the first step to being open to feedback. Receiving, and then applying that feedback, is like being given a key to unlock all the doors that have been previously closed.

Exercise: Being Curious

This week, here are some ways to practice being curious:

- Whenever you are confronted with a negative thought or a belief that holds you back, ask yourself these questions:
  - What if that weren't true?
  - What if I did it a different way?
  - What if I gave it a second shot?
  - What is the worst thing that could happen?

- When a feeling of resistance or anger arises, can you recognize the feeling and name it? For example, "I feel angry" or "I am feeling some resistance; I don't want to change." Dig a little deeper and ask yourself, "Why do I feel angry? Where is this coming from? What fears do I have? What stories am I telling myself? Are these stories true? What proof do I have that they are true?"

- Over the next week, when someone offers advice, really listen while they are talking. Don't prepare your response—just listen. Ask them "Tell me more" and allow yourself to be open to their ideas and feedback. Avoid responding or discounting their argument or point of view, even in your inside voice.

- Get outside your typical routine. Revisit a topic or field of interest you once explored, but thought you hated. Could you give it another shot? If you didn't like reading books when you were younger, try listening to audiobooks or joining a book club for social interaction and accountability. Perhaps listen to a podcast by one of your favorite thought leaders. Is there an area of interest you were once passionate about but have since lost focus as your career progressed? Try revisiting it. Or is there an outlier—some field you never considered before (think Meghan and the non-profit)—that you could try? Ask yourself, what would my life look like if I tried X? Revisit your transferable skills from last week; what jobs might they apply to that you hadn't considered?

- Practice saying "You might be right" in conversations throughout the week. When someone presents information that you may automatically disagree with, repeat these four words and ask them to explain. Listen to understand, and let go of the need to be right or to explain your position. How does the conversation go? Did you notice any changes? Did you learn anything new?

RECEIVING AND APPLYING FEEDBACK

Everything that irritates us about others can lead us
to an understanding of ourselves.

— Carl Jung

IT'S NOT PERSONAL, IT'S BUSINESS.

In John Huston's film *Prizzi's Honor*, a mob hit man played by Jack Nicholson balks at killing his wife until his father explains, "It's just business, Charlie!"[1]

The iconic line has been used many times in other films—and in offices everywhere. We've also heard "It's not personal, it's just business," usually at a point when someone doesn't want us to take offense to what they just said. But when it comes to receiving feedback, criticism, or reviews, we can't help but take it personally.

A few years ago, someone we hired wasn't performing and I needed to address it. Let's just say she didn't respond to my feedback with curiosity. "Do you know how much education I have? Do you know how much I have done for this company?" she replied. In her mind, everything she did was perfect and no one around her knew nearly as much as she did. However, according to my executive team, she was falling short in at least five areas. The feedback was unanimous. This wasn't just a case of someone not getting along with her—this was a case in which everyone agreed she was falling short.

As I tried to explain what changes we wanted to see, she became angry. I knew the discussion had to change, so I said: "I am trying to help you be better."

Candace often sees this kind of defensiveness in her coaching practice. Clients come to her and explain how much they know, how credentialed they are, how many degrees they have, and how many hours they work. It's a common refrain: "How can they tell me that I'm doing it wrong when they see me working so hard? I work harder than everyone else!"

OUR PERCEPTION ISN'T REALITY.

What Candace hears when she listens to these complaints is that something isn't adding up. That is, sometimes how we see ourselves is not how we're seen by others. Often we have blind spots about how we are perceived. We have no idea people think of us as a "know-it-all," "a flake," "the office mom," "incompetent," etc. We tend to look at ourselves through rose-colored glasses, and everyone else with a magnifying glass. We can so clearly point out the flaws in others, but we can't see them in ourselves. This is precisely why 360-degree feedback reviews can be helpful. When multiple people say the same thing about your performance, it's hard to argue. And it can become a teaching tool, rather than a punitive one.

Sometimes people focus on the wrong skills or attributes. They may have a specialty or be good at a certain job task. For example, a lawyer can know everything about the law but might be terrible at communicating or litigating. A doctor can know his profession inside out but have a terrible bedside manner. A salesperson can be persuasive but unethical. Both realities can exist simultaneously. Candace once had a manager who focused on the details but couldn't see the big picture. She was failing miserably at managing, but her spreadsheets and forms were works of art. "How can you criticize me for this? Nobody else can do what I do here!" And she was right, nobody could do spreadsheets the way she could. But it didn't matter how great she was at this because she wasn't being paid to make spreadsheets. She was being paid to manage people.

The Spreadsheet Queen isn't alone. It's easy to lose sight of the forest for the trees in any profession. It's human nature to focus on and excel at the tasks we have a natural affinity and talent for. However, we have to be mindful that most professions require us to be proficient in multiple roles. And it follows that we will have areas in constant need of improvement. The key is to be prepared to listen to what others have to say, and to be open and curious, rather than defensive and furious.

> "Whenever you are about to find fault with someone,
> ask yourself the following question: What fault of mine
> most nearly resembles the one I am about to criticize?"
>
> —**Marcus Aurelius,** *Meditations*

HOW TO STOP TAKING THINGS PERSONALLY

I recently had to confront an employee who was working too much. She was in the office twelve hours a day, six days a week. I also noticed tall piles of papers and folders on her desk. From my perspective, the job she was tasked with shouldn't take more than forty hours and she needed help organizing as well as managing her time. I could tell she was burning out. When I offered her help, her response wasn't what I expected. Instead of being grateful, she broke down in tears. "I work so hard, and nobody appreciates me!" She had interpreted my help as criticism.

I had to correct her and say, "No! That's not true. People absolutely appreciate your effort. We think we could help you use your team and some new technology that is available to you to make your life better."

She was resistant. The more I listened to her, the clearer the picture became. I could see that *she didn't want* to get rid of the piles of work. She wanted everyone to see how busy she was and how much work she had to do. Deep down she told herself the story that she would only be valuable if she was "busy." She also had a bit of a martyr complex. She saw herself as someone who was making sacrifices for the team; the whole operation would collapse without her. The interesting thing about martyrs is they act like they aren't getting anything for all their troubles and sacrifices, but indeed they are. This person enjoyed the attention the piles of work brought to her. Unfortunately, it was the wrong kind of attention. And instead of reaping any real rewards or benefits, all she reaped was resentment and anger. Her behavior and energy brought the rest of the team down.

Have you ever been around someone who constantly huffs and sighs, and acts annoyed? (Candace calls this the "martyr mutter.") They are exhausting to be around. You may even be afraid to ask them to do anything—a bonus for some martyr mutterers. Who can forget when *Seinfeld*'s George Costanza figured out this trick: as long as he was sighing, shaking his head, and running around the office appearing stressed, no one asked him to do any work.

My employee didn't see how her actions affected the entire team. All she could see was her vantage point, misguided though it was. In fact, if I asked anyone on the team whether they thought she was proficient, highly valuable, and a hard worker, they wouldn't agree with her self-assessment. To someone else, she looked incapable of managing her basic tasks.

If she could move past the story she told herself and be open to hearing feedback, she might recognize that she didn't need to work herself into the ground to be seen as valuable. If she grew curious and asked some of the questions we proposed last week—*What if appearing constantly busy didn't make me more valuable? What if it's making me seem less competent? What if I did my work differently?*—she could open up to learning new skills and tools. Another question she could have asked herself was: *What if I tried it Chris's way for a bit?* And then: *What would my life look like if I didn't work seventy hours a week? What else could I do with my time?* Those questions would have allowed her to imagine a different way of working.

Unfortunately, this employee dug her heels into the sand. As time went on, she only grew more and more defensive. She had written her story and it was the hill she would die on. It was also a self-fulfilling prophecy. After a while, no one wanted to work with her. Imagine how difficult it is to work with someone who feels perpetually undervalued and underappreciated. They resent everyone they work with and make everyone around them walk on eggshells. No one felt free to ask this employee to do anything without feeling they would somehow be indebted to her. She also picked fights with everyone, even our CIO. We began to think she was hoping to get fired. And that's ultimately what happened. She set out to prove everyone "hated her" and that's exactly what she made happen.

When I originally spoke with her, I urged her to not let her story define her. I let her know she had an entire team who was willing to help her. I warned her that sending emails at 11:30 p.m. did not prove what a good worker she was, and it didn't endear her to others who valued their off-work hours. I told her that the perception she hoped to achieve wasn't her reality. She refused to believe it.

So many people come into my office and tell me (in other words, tell themselves—I'm just the audience) stories that cast them as the hero or the victim. Those who believe they are victims act as if they are powerless to change anything, including their own behavior, and are always the most resistant to feedback. Conversely, those who cast themselves as heroes are equally resistant to change. It's only those who are ready to hear feedback, to respond and change their behavior, who can see themselves as simply an "actor" in their story—not the victim, the villain, or hero. They are there to do whatever is necessary, no matter what "lines" are thrown their way or what the "comments from the margins" are in the ongoing story of their life.

Unfortunately, this story doesn't have a happy ending. (I do wish her the best wherever she is.) But I tell this story as a cautionary tale. She didn't read the room. She was blind to how her behavior affected others. She believed in her own reality so much that she missed the clues around her. People weren't going to go out of their way to say, "thank you" and to appreciate her (which is what she was hoping for) because they perceived her as disorganized and inefficient—the exact opposite of the persona she thought she had created. *They didn't like how she made them feel.* This is something many of us underestimate: People will put up with a lot of things, but they won't put up with being cast as the villain in a story they didn't write.

HOW TO READ THE ROOM

Everyone needs feedback. So many people are unaware of how their behavior, words, and actions impact others. Feedback helps us become aware of what we can't see in or about ourselves. And sometimes that feedback is silent, hinted at in subtle cues and responses. You don't want to be hauled into a boss's office or HR to find out the hard way. It's best to be on the lookout for subtle (and sometimes not so subtle) clues on how you impact others. And the best way to do this is to learn how to read the room.

We all know people who pride themselves on being excellent speakers—they believe everyone is dying to hear their latest story, but they can't read the room. They miss the knowing glances that seem to say, "Here he goes again." They don't notice someone trying to escape the conversation. They ignore how a person checks their phone, their watch, or avoids eye contact. Sometimes they stay, but they roll their eyes, shuffle their feet, or barely repress a sigh—all obvious tells—if you're looking for them.

Learning to watch others for nonverbal cues is just as important as listening to them. Many times people are afraid to say what they want to out loud, but their behavior speaks volumes. Are people always "too busy" to stop and talk to you in the hallway? Do they have other commitments or plans when you reach out? Do you feel left out of meetings, conferences, lunches, and after work get-togethers?

Chances are people have a different perception of you than you do. If you can't make heads or tails of it, it's time to be proactive and *ask for feedback*. While this can be uncomfortable, it shows a courageous willingness to learn and grow. And it may invite some much-needed perspective. Feedback doesn't have to be contentious; it can be a learning experience. Assure the person you ask for feedback that you are going to listen to them and give what they have to say serious consideration. And then *listen*.

WHEN LISTENING IS DIFFICULT—MANAGING EMOTIONAL RESPONSES TO FEEDBACK

If you find yourself reacting to feedback—that is, having a visceral, physical reaction while listening—then you may need to step back and take a deep breath. What's a visceral, physical reaction to feedback? Some people might sweat or feel a pit in the bottom of their stomach. Others might dissociate, as though they can't hear anything that's being said. When this happens, it's time to pause. Recognize that you are having an emotional reaction to feedback, which is completely normal. Everyone does. Some people feel this way even BEFORE they hear feedback. Just the mere words "We need to talk" can trigger an anxious reaction—am I right?

When Candace, a self-professed recovering "apple polisher" and "Straight-A student," first entered the workforce, she entered almost every feedback session wired for a fight. "I couldn't even hear the words my boss was saying, I was so anxious." Even though she knew she was doing a great job, she feared being called out for mistakes she might have made. "I could be three-quarters of the way through the review when I realized I hadn't heard a thing."

The fear of disappointing someone, of failure, of making a mistake, or being perceived as less than perfect can make anyone feel anxious. It's true for almost everyone that "if it's hysterical, it's historical." What that means is that many of us have previous negative experiences associated with feedback. Perhaps a parent yelled or berated us as a kid when we messed up. Maybe a harsh teacher humiliated us in front of our classmates. Or a coach repeatedly called us out and made the team suffer for our mistakes. A loved one constantly criticized us. Nothing we did was good enough. We all have physical responses to feedback. On the surface, hearing a boss say we need to improve or something needs to change can feel harmless, but our body keeps the score. When we feel threatened, it activates the fight-or-flight response within our brain.

We sometimes forget that we're human beings when we enter these conversations—bosses included, as I can personally attest. Most bosses expect others to hear every word they say, to take their advice and be grateful for it. The reality is a lot more nuanced than that. We are ALL emotional beings, and our feelings can get the better of us.

A universally acknowledged tool in deescalating an employee's emotional response is something called the R.A.I.N technique. R.A.I.N. is an acronym for a mindfulness technique that helps to:

> **Recognize** what is happening (what is the emotion?).
>
> **Allow** the experience to be there (not force it or fight it, which makes it worse).
>
> **Investigate** with curiosity, and then . . .
>
> **Non-identify** (or de-personalize).

Recognize the emotion.

When a feeling arises in the middle of receiving feedback, simply recognize and label the emotion. Naming or recognizing a feeling activates the logical center of your brain, the prefrontal cortex. It literally turns off the emotional response center and turns on the rational thinking center. Of course, if you're in the middle of the feedback session, you'll want to do this exercise quietly. Internally you may think, "Wow, I am shocked." Or "I am really angry." Or "I am so disappointed." Or "I am ashamed." A common one, the most prevalent, is "I am afraid." Statements like "I am anxious" or "I feel threatened" tell your brain what is happening. It helps you get past the feeling.

If you feel comfortable with the person you're speaking with, it's perfectly okay to ask, "May I have a moment? I am feeling a bit anxious, and I'd like to be able to focus on and hear what you have to say." This brings you back to the present moment, and it invites both you and the person who's giving you feedback to slow down and not get swept up in emotion. If they are adept they might say, "I see you're anxious. Let's take getting suspended or fired off the table. That's not happening today." Most people go to the worst-case scenario when anxious and immediately assume the worst. Even if you don't hear someone say, "You're not getting fired today," remind yourself that is likely not going to happen every time you receive feedback.

Allow the experience.

Most of the pain and anxiety we feel is in our mind. We tell ourselves a story, and then we believe that version of events. We fight any version of that story that is in opposition to our own beliefs. By allowing the experience to unfold, you stop fighting and resisting what is happening and surrender to *what is*. It allows you to hear the other person's perspective. It allows you to focus on the experience. It gets you out of your head and into the moment at hand. It sets your mind up to get curious, rather than spiraling and preparing to fight, run out of the room, freeze, or dissociate altogether.

Investigate with curiosity.

There's that word again. By investigating and getting curious about how you feel, you can purposefully dull the emotional impact. By asking questions, you disarm the person giving you feedback. Statements like "Help me understand your point of view" or "I feel differently, but I am willing to listen to your feelings on the matter" go a long way. By seeking to understand, rather than proving who is right or wrong, you give yourself the space to take in more information. You may still be upset, but you won't let your emotions take over.

Candace recommends bringing a notebook into meetings. "It's like going to a doctor. If you've ever received a scary diagnosis, it's incredibly difficult to remember anything that was said after the words, 'You have cancer.'" Writing things down not only helps you remember, but it also helps you to deescalate. The more you take notes, the more you engage the logical center of your brain, and the less likely you'll be to block things out or react emotionally. Having prepared questions helps too. One question Candace recommends asking is, "Can I get back to you in a couple of days and tell you what my plan is for (making improvement) or doing it differently?" This way, you don't have to react in the meeting or invent a plan on the spot. Sometimes it may even be appropriate to schedule the meeting for another time. For example, "I am not really ready to respond today. May I have a couple of days to think about it and get back to you?" Sometimes waiting twenty-four to forty-eight hours to respond can help you see things more clearly. Another tip Candace shares is to thank the person when receiving their feedback—recognize that it was vulnerable and sometimes scary for the person to be honest and open. Something as simple as "Thank you for trusting me enough to tell me the truth" or "Thank you for helping me. I know this wasn't easy for you either" lets the person giving the feedback know you heard and understood the feedback was meant to help.

Non-Identify.

One way to think about non-identifying with an emotion is to not "be the emotion." Emotions are temporary. We *feel* happy, but we *aren't* happy 24/7. We *feel* anxious for a time, but we *aren't* anxious every minute of every day. We fail and make mistakes, but that doesn't mean we *are* failures. It is only by recognizing that feelings and emotions aren't fixed states that we are able to move past them. We can't have clear, honest, and fruitful conversations if we're stuck in a feeling; this commits us to "being" this feeling—anxious, angry, upset, righteous, etc.—forever. To truly hear the information that will help us improve, we must be in an open state of mind that allows for this to occur. And the best way to do this is by taking the emotion out of the conversation. In other words, to depersonalize the feedback.

Depersonalizing criticism means recognizing that every person, no matter how brilliant or talented, needs someone to provide honest, clear, and unbiased feedback. This doesn't mean there is something wrong with you; it means you need to work on some aspect of your job or performance. And you aren't alone.

Michael Jordan, one of the greatest basketball players of all time, relied on his coach, Phil Jackson, for feedback. And Jordan is not an outlier. Every single NFL, NBA, MLB, and professional athlete has a coach. Every actress and actor on the screen or stage—Oscar and Tony winners included—has a director who gives them notes on their performance in real time. If you leave your office, walk down the street, and step foot into any establishment, every person you meet has received some sort of feedback about their performance. I would even say that the more positive, efficient, and productive the person you meet is, the more feedback they have received and applied over time.

LIGHTEN UP: DON'T TAKE YOURSELF TOO SERIOUSLY.

This isn't something you learn in college, but you can't take everything, including yourself, too seriously. Yes, your job is serious business. But it's okay to take a deep breath and laugh at your mistakes. One thing that has always helped Candace and me is humor. In the middle of a feedback session, Candace recommends poking a little fun at yourself.

"So does this mean my Yelp score just went down half a star?"

This isn't being snarky, defensive, or even dismissive. This simple statement acknowledges that your performance wasn't "five-star" but it's not life-altering. It doesn't put you at the bottom of the proverbial "recommended employee" list. It diffuses the tension and takes the pressure off the person giving the feedback. It also demonstrates that you acknowledge room for improvement. You're not defensive, contrarian, or closed to hearing more. It invites a new level of intimacy too. Humor can be disarming. Consider following this up with, "So what would an employee have to do to get a five-star Yelp review?"

ASKING FOR AND GIVING FEEDBACK

A feedback session doesn't have to be painful. In fact, feedback is best when it is consistent and more frequent. Many Gen Z and Millennials report wanting more feedback; they want to know what they can do to improve their performance. According to a study conducted by gen-WHY, a Communication Strategy firm that specializes in employee retention for Millennials and Gen Z, 69 percent of employees preferred to receive feedback weekly or even more frequently![2] Some even preferred daily feedback. Gen X and Boomers aren't accustomed to this frequency and may balk at this. It might even feel excessive to those of us accustomed to one annual review (if that). But this is a generation that grew up with online reviews. Gen Z and Millennials review every purchase, movie, television show, app, and experience. And they aren't shy about sharing their opinions. Gen Z and Millennials prefer immediate (and digital) feedback.

To be relevant in today's workplace, you need to be able to respond and adapt to current, consistent modes of communication. Products such as Microsoft Teams, Slack, and other project platforms are common in offices now, and keep a team more connected than ever. In my company, we conduct post-mortem reviews after we complete each project. I think the days of annual reviews as the only time to get and give feedback are gone. If you want to be relevant and stay relevant, you need to be adept at asking for it and giving it consistently—just not when a problem arises. This means getting comfortable with asking for and receiving feedback rather than waiting for it. Whether you do that daily, weekly, monthly, or quarterly, or after a project is up to you.

FEEDBACK DOESN'T HAVE TO BE NEGATIVE.

We often assume that feedback is always negative, but this couldn't be further from the truth. The best feedback helps others build the skills and talents that already work for them. We all need to be better at catching people doing good work, so much of which goes unnoticed. The squeaky wheel truly does get the grease. (If you're under the age of thirty, that means "the problems get all the attention.")

When you seek advice and feedback from others, also ask them what you do *well*. What areas are working for you? Similarly, think about whether you consistently provide helpful and positive feedback. Or do you wait for a problem to arise first? If you want to be relevant, be of service to others. Show that you are truly looking out for others and willing to help them in their careers. See the good in them and use your positive feedback to help them flourish.

Now, this may not always work. Remember, some people are committed to their own stories. You can't raise the bar for someone who is clinging to the bottom rung and claiming everyone is enjoying stepping on their hands.

ONE MORE THING—SAY THANK YOU.

Don't forget—it's not easy for someone to give feedback, offer advice, or suggest improvements. Think of the last time you had to tell someone they were doing a task incorrectly or that their behavior was disruptive or hurtful. How did you feel at that moment? No one wants to be the bad guy. (As a parent, I know that feeling well.) You can't expect everyone to like you or to hear everything you have to say—but sometimes you have to say it anyway, for their own good. When someone is courageous and brave enough to have a difficult conversation with you, acknowledge how difficult it must be for them and don't forget to thank them. This shows incredible grace and your willingness to change. It's also rarely done, so if you want to stand out, thank someone for their feedback—whether it's positive or negative. Or go a step further and send a handwritten note. Talk about making a lasting impression!

As my stories in this chapter attest, not everyone is great at accepting feedback, and most of us don't find it a pleasant experience. But what separates the greatest athletes, performers, and employees from the rest is the ability to receive feedback and improve upon it. Those who are able to overcome their discomfort and remain open to feedback are the successful employees who others see as coachable, adaptable, and curious. It's the secret weapon to improving performance.

EXERCISES: HOW TO HANDLE FEEDBACK

Author Stephen Covey was the first to point out that "we judge ourselves by our intentions and others by their behavior."[3] That means we often feel misunderstood and unfairly criticized. While we may understand our intentions, we can't control how others perceive us. For this exercise, put yourself in the place of someone who is giving you feedback. If you did not know anything about what you intended, how would your actions come across?

Shift the focus of the conversation to the other person. If you're getting feedback about a specific incident, look at what happened as if you were watching a movie. You can see what the character (you) is doing, but not why. When you strip away your internal story about what happened, you can start to see how someone else would view it. *Perhaps your body language was aggressive. You interrupted her three times. You dismissed his concerns before you'd given them thought.*

Viewing yourself as a character in the movie (without casting yourself as the hero or victim) might give you a different perspective. To avoid coming across as defensive, don't keep the conversation about only you. Turn the discussion to the other person, too. This allows them to speak their mind. That way, both of you can move forward in a different, and hopefully more positive, direction.

- Experiment with the power of "What if?" The next time you receive feedback, and you feel defensive, try this instead: Ask yourself, "What if they are right/this is true?" You don't have to accept it as an objective fact; just try it on like a hat. Look in the mirror and see if it fits.

- Then ask yourself: "If this is true, what would it mean?" Consider how your actions/speech/decisions might affect others.

- Prepare in advance when you want to give feedback to someone. Write down the advice or the story you want to tell as you would say it. Then read it out loud. How does it sound?

- Now write it down in a completely different way. You might change "The way you plan to approach this issue won't work" to "Tell me how you decided on this course of action. What other alternatives did you consider?" Or even, "How certain are you that this is the right approach? Do you have a contingency plan in case A, B, or C happens?"

- And finally, ask, "How can I help you with this? Do you see a role for me to play here?"

MINDSET SELF-ASSESSMENT

If you're reading this book straight through, then you've been working on your coachability, adaptability, curiosity, and openness to feedback. If you've completed the assessments and exercises along the way, you may have noticed a shift (or two) in how you think about yourself and how you approach others. Let's take some time to look at the progress you've made and what still needs work.

On a scale of 1 to 5, with 1 being the least true and 5 being the most true, how would you rate yourself after four weeks of thoughtful focus?

1. I feel more adaptable. I feel more confident that whatever happens, I will be able to handle it and even thrive.

   1   2   3   4   5

2. I know where my performance could be stronger, and I have set a goal to improve.

   1   2   3   4   5

3. I am actively seeking coaching to improve my performance.

    1   2   3   4   5

4. I am more open to hearing what people have to say; I feel less defensive.

    1   2   3   4   5

5. I am more in control of my emotional response to criticism and to other people's mistakes. I take time to become curious rather than furious.

    1   2   3   4   5

6. I use my curiosity to understand what people are trying to tell me. I ask questions and listen to the answers.

    1   2   3   4   5

7. I have changed my feedback to others to be more curious, empathetic, and forward-thinking (focused on solutions rather than blame).

    1   2   3   4   5

Write down a brief description of a time you practiced your new mindset and what happened. We know it's important to log small (or big!) victories so you can remember and reflect on them.

Now for the hard part . . .

Choose a trusted teammate, friend, or mentor to give you feedback based on the preceding statements and scales. Select someone who knows you, has your best interest at heart, and who will give you honest feedback.

Ask them to use the form on our website to complete this evaluation. After they finish the form, set a meeting time where the two of you can discuss how closely your rating (above) and their observations (the form) aligned. Note any discrepancies and use them as an opportunity to practice openness, curiosity, and a willingness to receive feedback. Use specific examples (both positive and not so positive) of your behavior and dig deep into how you've improved (or where you need to).

Remember: Thank them for their feedback and the time they took to share it with you.

Your Plan

1. The hardest mindset change for me has been:

_____

_____

_____

_____

2. The mindset issues I'm still working on are:

_____

_____

_____

_____

Review the mindset exercises every few months and record your progress.

MONTH TWO

Skillset Practices

Nobody ever mastered any skills except through
intensive persistent and intelligent practice.

—Norman Vincent Peale

Y ou've spent the past few weeks getting to know yourself, what makes you tick, the stories you tell yourself, and how to become more coachable, adaptable, curious, and receptive to feedback. Now that you have your mindset straight, the rest is gravy, right? You know better now, so of course you'll do better!

If only life—change—were that easy!

INSIGHT DOESN'T ALWAYS LEAD TO BEHAVIOR CHANGE.

If there is one thing I have learned in the past two and half decades working with and leading others, it's that insight doesn't always lead to change. I can't tell you how many times I have had meaningful and profound conversations with people who sincerely promised to change, but for one reason or another they couldn't deliver on that promise. Just because they were aware of a problematic behavior or bad decision didn't mean they were ready to make lasting changes.

There is no better example of this than the man who made a lifetime study of human thinking, psychoanalyst Sigmund Freud. Considered the founder of psychoanalysis, Freud developed many groundbreaking insights into the workings of the human mind, particularly regarding the role of the unconscious and the impact of early childhood experiences on later behaviors in adulthood. However, despite his deep understanding of the human psyche, Freud struggled with harmful personal behaviors and habits throughout his adult life. For example, even though Freud, a smoker, knew about the harmful effect smoking had on his health, he found he couldn't break his addictive habit. He smoked against the counsel of doctors and despite developing oral cancer. Knowing something is harmful, strangely, isn't enough to get us to stop doing it!

This is the hard part. Most of us *know* what we need to change, yet few of us are able to commit to the necessary behavioral changes. For example, there are many self-destructive behaviors that hold us back at work. Perhaps you interrupt people when they are talking because you're excited to speak and share genuine interest. You've been told it's disruptive or rude, but you just can't help yourself. Of course, that's an innocuous example, but there are more extreme examples. In the TV show *Mad Men*, the character of Don Draper has several moments of self-awareness: He knows that lying about his identity and his advertising credentials, not to mention his extramarital affairs and alcoholism, is self-destructive. Yet, throughout the series he fails to make any lasting change. Instead, he repeats the same self-destructive patterns despite his awareness. Tony Soprano, the lead character of the TV show *The Sopranos*, is in therapy where he gains insight into his mob-boss ways and the impact his mindset, behavior, and actions have on others. But he doesn't become an angel after learning what he needs to do to change. There's a reason we find these characters so compelling—they remind us that, as Candace says, "knowing doesn't always lead to growing."

> "Not everything that is faced can be changed, but
> nothing can be changed until it is faced."

—James Baldwin

Fortunately, most of us don't suffer from such severe human lapses. But deep inside, you might know exactly what is holding you back, even if you can't seem to flip the switch and make a consistent effort to change. Perhaps you don't listen well; you rush to finish your work and miss important details; you're bad at taking direction; you lack initiative and have trouble focusing; you're scared to speak up, take the lead, or try new things. These are just a few insights you might have gained along the way when examining your mindset.

And if you still don't know what has to change, there may be other indicators that what you're doing isn't working. Perhaps you're not getting called back on interviews; you're getting passed over for promotion; or you're not seen and appreciated at work the way you deserve to be. There are always outward signs that what you're doing isn't working.

Now that you're open to receiving those signs, it's time to do the heavy lifting.

FROM INSIGHT TO CHANGED BEHAVIOR

The key to ensuring lasting change is to develop a set of reinvention skills that push you past insight and into consistent effort. In the past weeks, we covered coachability, adaptability, curiosity, and the ability to receive feedback, but in the weeks ahead we will also require you to go beyond mere understanding. This is a different skillset than those discussed previously (such as hard and soft skills).

In the chapters to come, you'll develop the skills to help you *constantly reinvent yourself*, so that you always remain relevant. At every stage in your career, you'll know your values, as well as your employer's, within the job market and will use those values to reframe your story and build a record of excellence that sets you apart. With these skills, you'll be relevant at every stage of your career, anywhere you go.

WEEK 5

IDENTIFY YOUR NEEDS, VALUES, EXPECTATIONS, AND NON-NEGOTIABLES

When your values are clear to you,
making decisions becomes easier.

—Roy E. Disney

The best way to make a change is by taking meaningful action every day. What do I mean by meaningful action? For me, meaningful action means taking a step *forward*—a step toward progress on your goals. So many people think they are working toward their goals when they are just spinning in circles. I have known many people who think they are making progress because they are taking action. But the action they take is meaningless because they don't understand the role their values play in a satisfying career. The first step in moving toward your goals, then, is identifying your values.

Most people don't know their values, what their priorities are, or what they expect. They have set themselves on an impossible course and so they are always disappointed. I met one person who wanted to be a social worker . . . but who also wanted a house on the water, a boat, and weekends, evenings, and summers off to travel the world. From the sound of it, he prioritized a pretty upscale lifestyle. However, boats, a house on the beach, and expensive trips don't come cheaply or without sacrifice. What he prioritizes is the finer things in life, but he is not going to find this (or be able to afford this) if he wants a career as a social worker. That's not judgment; he's entitled to desire these things. But he also has to understand that what he prioritizes and the job he feels he will offer the most value are incompatible. He needs to reassess his needs, values, and non-negotiables.

UNDERSTANDING YOUR NEEDS, VALUES, AND NON-NEGOTIABLES

So many people are stuck because they don't understand how their financial needs, values, and non-negotiables relate to their career. Basing your career decisions and goals on your values will help you feel more fulfilled and able to reach your full potential. However, most of us can't do this unless our basic needs are met first. You may have heard of Maslow's hierarchy of needs, a motivational theory in psychology that consists of a five-tier model that leads to self-actualization. It's typically drawn or represented as a pyramid. At the base of the pyramid are the basics humans need to survive—like food, water, and decent shelter. These needs must be met before any other needs can be fulfilled. What does this have to do with work? Most of us work to meet our basic needs—we need to feed and clothe ourselves, and we need a home to live in. If we're not making enough to make ends meet—to meet these basic needs—then we can't focus on personal fulfillment and long-term goals. We're stuck living day to day and paycheck to paycheck. Every worker's priority is to have enough to live on.

After securing the bottom level of the pyramid (having our survival needs met), we next need to achieve a sense of safety and security. We need to trust that when we leave our home, we're safe from harm; that our property, and family, will remain safe while we go about our daily life. It also means we have money in the bank for a rainy day or can save for retirement or our kids' education. We need predictability—knowing what to expect from the people around us and our employers.

Once we have those two levels of needs met, we can then focus on friendship, relationships, and connection—building lasting bonds with others. That's why getting along with your team at the office matters—they are part of the connection we need to feel that we belong. We spend a good part of our waking hours at work, so feeling like an outsider can make you miserable, no matter how competent you may be at your job.

After all these needs have been met, we can work on our self-esteem—confidence, achievement, respect for others (it takes confidence to understand that other people's achievements don't diminish yours) and becoming proud of our individual identities, even the quirks. Only then can we "self-actualize," and by self-actualize I mean live according to your values, act creatively, find purpose and meaning, and live up to your potential.

What does it mean to self-actualize and fully live according to one's values? Candace, for example, needs to be able to do creative work with a minimum of oversight. Many years ago, she chose to work at a relatively small nonprofit so that she could be independent and know that her work had an impact on the organization. She was implementing her own ideas, and that was far more important to her than how much she earned. Candace was able to do this because: 1) her basic needs were met and 2) she understood her values. She knew that autonomy and creativity were critical to her happiness at work. She could never be happy working in a large corporate structure simply executing orders or writing mindless copy for someone else.

As Candace once explained to me, "I wanted to be able to define what the work was and how it needed to be done. Because I had proved my value and judgment to my boss, he allowed me to be in charge. I produced concepts and drafts for my boss, the CEO, and he gave feedback, which worked well for us both. Though I worked for the CEO, I was stationed in a different county, near the media, City Hall, and other essential partners. That also gave me the freedom to come and go as needed and only confer with the CEO when it was important (or just fun bonding)."

Candace knew she needed creative control to feel fulfilled and satisfied at work. "I love being the idea person," she explained. "I was able to be in on the start of new initiatives and projects we'd never done before, so I had the fun of brainstorming and organizing how a project needed to be designed to be successful. Someone else—lots of someones, with different skillsets—did the implementation." Candace understood her values and she built her career around them by taking action each day in alignment with those values. She has built her entire career path on these values: In 2020 she left full-time work and now works for a variety of clients, writing projects she enjoys for clients she respects, and she does all of it from her home office. She has time for all the things that matter to her, including working on passion projects.

Autonomy and creativity are examples of two values. You may share these values with Candace, but there are certainly others that may matter more.

The following is a list of values (it is by no means exhaustive) broken down by cultural, environmental, and workplace. Use this list to help you identify your values:

Cultural:

- Do you want to work for a company with a corporate culture that values a bias toward action, appreciation for your work, friendly workspaces?

- One that is open to new ideas and innovation?

Environmental:

- Do you value working in aesthetically pleasing spaces, having a short commute, working from home, or having access to high-end technology?

- Do you want to work in a bustling city, where you can step out during your lunch and explore, or do you prefer working in an office in the suburbs (close to home) or the country?

- Or are you an outdoorsy person, who couldn't imagine working in an office five days a week?

The Workplace:

- Do you enjoy and value helping people or making a difference in the world?

- Or do you value creating order from chaos, building or making things that matter, solving difficult problems?

- Do you value organizing and analyzing complex information?

- Or is connecting with or entertaining people important to you? Maybe it's educating people?

- Some people simply enjoy achieving their own personal goals and want to have more time to work on their own passion projects. Does that sound like you?

Work-Life Balance:

- Do you value work-life balance, such as spending time with your family without feeling guilty?

- Or does moving up in the company and progressing toward management or the C-suite, working long hours, but earning more, interest you?

- Do you enjoy more responsibility, learning new skills, taking on new projects, being able to mentor or support others, and winning awards or being the best at something?

Only you can answer these questions and know what resonates with you. Once you find what values matter *to you*, you're halfway there. The key, Candace advises, is to be able to do work that aligns with your values and to make sure these values *are also relevant for others, such as your manager and the company.*

For example, Candace values independence and autonomy. How does she demonstrate to her managers or bosses that these values benefit them? She tells/shows them. "By taking initiative, I am saving my boss time and energy from having to manage me carefully and frequently. And having high-end tech means I'm more efficient, can get more done, and stay connected better. Because I also value ambition, I am comfortable taking on more important work, bringing in more revenue or recognition for the company," she says. Another example of her values as a benefit to the company: "By valuing constantly learning new skills (and hiring great help), I developed deep skillsets in-house so my company doesn't need to hire consultants—saving them time and money."

UNDERSTAND AN ORGANIZATION'S VALUES

Once you understand your values and how they relate to your manager, it's imperative that those values align with your workplace or where you want to be hired. I have worked with hundreds of organizations over the years, and while many companies have their own unique set of values, many of their core priorities overlap. Understanding your values is important, but understanding what *an organization* values so that you can be sure you're the right fit is equally important. Most companies are quite clear about what they value; they usually include the language in their job descriptions or on the company's website (on the mission and corporate recruiting pages).

Here are just a few examples of what companies value:

Performance—and therefore pay commensurate with that performance.

Appreciation—and as a result, rewarding employees for efforts (sometimes monetary compensation, but also verbal or written recognition).

Opportunities for Advancement—Many companies reward employees and have a system in place that recognizes commitment to the company and to excellence—not just based on tenure or advanced degrees, but on actual performance.

Opportunities to Give Back—Many organizations believe in the importance of community involvement opportunities through work and fund-raising to support important causes.

Culture—This varies by company. Some companies boast an "entrepreneurial culture" that allows individuals the freedom to find their own "best practices." Others value a "team-oriented" approach, rather than an adversarial or competition-driven culture.

Diversity—I believe representation matters, and so do many prospective hires as well as those seeking advancement in an organization. In fact, many people rank this value as a priority. They believe organizations that hire and promote diverse individuals boost their overall "happiness" score in the workplace, especially when opportunities for advancement include everyone.

PRIORITIES VERSUS VALUES

Priorities are different from values. Values are fundamental beliefs that guide your decisions and actions. A priority is something that has established the right to a higher degree of importance or precedence. Many of us have similar values but different priorities. And priorities can change depending on one's circumstances. For example, two people can value performance and pay commensurate with performance, but each person can have different priorities depending on their life stage. A young person with two small children at home who needs childcare will value flexible scheduling, childcare at or near the office, and opportunities to work from home. Another person may prioritize advancement or opportunities to travel.

The prospective hires I speak to often have different priorities depending on where they are in their career. Your priorities may change over time; in fact, it's almost certain they will. Understanding what's most important to you right now will help you express your priorities—and how they affect what you're looking for—to your current or potential employer.

Here are some examples:

Family: If you have young children, older family members, or others who rely on you, you'll need to make sure you're there for them. Your priorities may include:

- Flexibility—the ability to pick up kids from school or daycare, or a flexible schedule that allows you to take family members to appointments or answer personal calls

- Work from home options
- Excellent medical benefits
- A short commute
- Little or no extended travel

Salary: If you're in your peak earning years (thirty to fifty years old, when you've got skills, experience, maturity, and a lot of energy and drive to succeed) you may prioritize compensation, especially if you are paying for college, buying a home, like to travel, or are saving for retirement (see below).

Retirement: If you're at the point in your career where you prioritize saving for retirement, you may place more emphasis on 401k plans or choosing a job where you can stay and thrive until your target retirement age.

Skills/Training: You may need to develop specific job skills or acquire certifications to stay relevant in your field. Some companies may have just the right role to give you that training, even if the job doesn't advance you in other ways.

Risk Aversion: In the workforce, there's actually no such thing as "job security," but there are some jobs that have less risk. For example: an established firm (low risk) versus a startup (higher risk); a government job (low risk) versus a grant-funded project (higher risk); an organization that's been growing steadily (low risk) for the past several years versus one that appears stagnant or in decline (higher risk)—no matter how appealing the role or salary. If avoiding risk is your priority, you can make informed decisions based on the factors that are right for you, rather than be taken in by shiny job offers.

Advancement: If your priority is to climb the corporate ladder, you'll need to understand how your current or future role will advance your career. Titles, salary, budget, prestige, and headcount may be factors in how you decide what role is the right one for you.

MANAGING YOUR EXPECTATIONS

If you're stuck, you may need to assess your expectations and to ask yourself: *What is the outcome I am looking for?* For some it may be income—the higher the income the better. But for many, income is just a slice of the whole pie. It may not even be the biggest piece. Do you want to be famous? Do you want to make a difference? Do you want to feel joy? Do you want to feel creative every day? Do you want to feel free or independent? What would it take for you to feel as though you were self-actualized and living to your highest potential? I think the best way to get in touch with your values is to ask yourself: *What do I really want?*

Your expectations determine your job satisfaction. As a career coach, Candace told her clients that "every job is someone else's dream job—even the one you're currently so anxious to leave." You could be working at a great job in a great company, but if the [salary/title/career path] doesn't meet your expectations, then you won't be happy. If your expectations aren't aligned with your current situation or your job goals—and values—then you'll be miserable and at risk of becoming irrelevant.

I see it all the time. Here are just a few examples:

- A young, fresh-out-of-college graduate who expects a big title and salary right away

- A mid-career manager who won't budge on travel, learning new skills, or changing their ways yet still expects to be promoted to the next level

- An applicant who's been out of the industry or the job market for years but who thinks they can walk back into their former role and title

- An applicant who changes careers or industries and expects their market value to remain the same

If you have specific expectations, you'll need to determine whether you're on the right path to achieve those outcomes. Are you willing to change the path you're on? Are you willing to put in the effort to achieve those goals?

If the answer is yes, and you can demonstrate that to an employer, you'll remain relevant and valuable to your team. But understand that what you want may take a while. Even if you're in the middle of your career and feel entitled to a higher income or a flashy title, you may not be able to achieve that right away, especially if you switch careers or industries. This is where patience and being comfortable with delayed gratification comes in handy.

If, for example, in the process of assessing your expectations and priorities, you discover that you don't want to be a social worker, but a sales professional, then you have to be willing to start at the bottom somewhere and work your way up. Your personal expectations are not the responsibility of your current or future employer; it's not the company's fault if you decide to switch careers. You will have to start over. The key is keeping your eyes on the goal.

UNDERSTANDING YOUR NON-NEGOTIABLES

Knowing what you want is important, but knowing what you can't tolerate is essential to your satisfaction at work. When you spot your non-negotiables in an interview or on the job, you'll recognize them as signs that you might want to move on.

Here are some examples I've heard over the years.

Your non-negotiables may be based on your priorities:

- I often hear that travel, relocation, a full-time office schedule, or a certain salary or title are "non-negotiable." I respect people's priorities, but I hope they'll see these not as yes/no propositions, but opportunities to negotiate. Consider traveling once or twice a year, for example, or remote work that requires visiting the office just a few days a month.

Your non-negotiables may also be cultural:

- Respect: Treating employees as expendable or not valuing their intelligence or contribution may be non-negotiable. A company that retains arrogant managers who talk down to their staff (or about their staff) sends a strong signal about how valuable their employees really are.

- How customers are treated: An organization that treats its [customers/patients/those they're paid to care for] poorly will eventually erode the humanity of those who work there.

- Micromanagement: A manager or company that can't trust its employees to do their jobs is saying more about their own trustworthiness.

- Stinginess in pay, recognition, technology, or even office supplies: These indicate that a company is either in trouble financially (a problem on a different level) or is telling its workforce they're not worthy of investment.

- Being untrustworthy. Managers or companies that say one thing and do another, or say they'll do something and never do, quickly lose the trust of their workers. Once trust is broken, everything is broken.

"You have more potential than you think, but you will never know your full potential unless you keep challenging yourself and pushing beyond your own self-imposed limits."

—Roy T. Bennett

SETTING REALISTIC EXPECTATIONS FOR YOURSELF

Once you understand your values, priorities, expectations, and non-negotiables, as well as those of the organization you hope to work for (or already do), it's time to be very honest about whether you're able to deliver. For example, say you have been hired for a job and it turns out, after some time, that you (or your employer) realize that you're not the best person for it. It takes courage to admit that you're not a good fit or that you're not living up to your fullest potential or the company's expectations. Maybe you don't really like the job you're doing, but you love the organization. You love the leadership, the culture, or what the company builds or creates. This is a place you can really shine.

This is when you need to have a tough conversation with your leader and say, "I really want to stay here, but the job I am doing doesn't align with my capabilities. I thought I was an autonomous person who liked to do behind-the-scenes work on my own, but it turns out, I need project-based work and more interaction with a team I enjoy."

It's a risk, of course. Not every company will have other opportunities available to you, but I recommend that you always start within your organization if you can, especially if you enjoy working there. If you're lucky enough to work in an organization that has a performance plan and is willing to help you improve and provide coaching or mentorship until you find a more suitable position, always stay in that company.

However, if the opposite is true—you love the role, but the company is not the right fit—then leave and find a place where you can really thrive and where your values are aligned with that of the company's.

Candace can speak to this firsthand. Many years ago, she worked in the technology department of a national company, a very large and established organization with a lot of old-school managers and detailed work. She felt like an anonymous cog in a giant machine with no recognition, no joy, and no end in sight. Candace was miserable, and she didn't feel she was adding value to the organization. And though she was capable and doing the job well, she was betraying her own values—autonomy and creativity—by staying there.

This is why becoming intimate with your values helps steer you onto a true career path. Along the way, you'll understand why you were unsuccessful or unhappy in those other jobs. Usually when a role doesn't work out in one organization it's because your values aren't aligned with those of the company's or your team's. It's important to take the time to assess and think about what it is you truly value before you move on, so you don't get stuck in the same way again.

VALUES THAT MAKE YOU
RELEVANT IN EVERY MARKET

Once you know your values, your organization's, and whether they align, it's time to figure out which values make you stand out in the job market. These are the values that are timeless and always relevant. For example, credibility (having integrity and being trustworthy), competence, and authenticity will endear you to any organization for the duration of your career.

> "The way to learn whether a person
> is trustworthy is to trust him."
>
> —**Ernest Hemingway**

Credibility

When you begin any position, it's nearly impossible to immediately show how credible and trustworthy you are. That's because building credibility takes time. You can only be deemed trustworthy when someone places their trust in you. You can only establish your credibility by creating a track record of delivering on your promises. Ask yourself the following questions (and answer honestly):

- Are you credible and trustworthy?

- Are your employers and/or the people you manage able to count on you to execute? Or do you often have excuses as to why things aren't completed?

- Do you show up late?

- Do you complete your projects in a timely manner?

- Do others constantly badger you to complete your tasks or micromanage to make sure your work is done correctly?

- How often in the past week, two weeks, month, or year, have you made an excuse for why something wasn't done?

- Are you honest? Do you tell people the truth?

- Do you lie about what you're doing or where you're going? Do you fudge your hours or expenses?

- Do you make up stories or pretend the work took longer than it did?

- Do you steal from the company—time, lunches, equipment, intellectual property, vacation time, sick time?

If you answered yes to any of these questions, you may think you are getting away with something. But someone always catches on, and this news will eventually make its way to the top. If you aren't credible, if your employers can't rely on you, they will eventually stop trusting you altogether.

"Everybody's got a different circle of competence.
The important thing is not how big the circle is.
The important thing is staying inside the circle."

—**Warren Buffett**

Competence

Doing a job well will never be underrated or undervalued. Become very good at what you do, even if that means doing something over and over, constantly improving and raising the bar—the not-so-fun parts of the job. Ask for feedback, seek a mentor, take on more responsibilities, do more than what is asked, and go above and beyond. A competent employee will always be valued—no matter where you go.

"Authenticity is a collection of choices that we have
to make every day. It's about the choice to show up
and be real. The choice to be honest. The choice to
let our true selves be seen."

—**Brené Brown**

Authenticity

Authenticity is one of the most difficult challenges in the modern workplace. When you are authentic, real, and vulnerable, you are unafraid to admit mistakes. You're courageous when it is time to speak up and you're okay with being judged because you've stood up for what is right or best for the company. You show courage when you've been called out as wrong or been disagreed with, but don't take it as a personal attack.

We live in a world influenced by social media, where everyone shows their highlight reels—not their mistakes, failures, or their worst days. However, it's the mistakes, failures, and moments of vulnerability where we learn the most. The actor George Clooney once said, "You learn nothing from success. . . . You learn everything from failing."[1]

As a leader, one of the values I treasure most is whether I can trust someone. I rely on people who tell me the truth and provide accurate data; people who are good at their jobs and aren't afraid to tell me what I need to hear. Trust, competency, and authenticity will always be valued in every workplace.

IT'S OKAY IF YOUR VALUES AND PRIORITIES CHANGE OVER TIME.

While I was writing this book, and specifically this chapter, something occurred to me. I realized that values and priorities evolve over time. What I valued and prioritized as a young man has changed considerably, and I am grateful for that.

Like many people I know, my core values were influenced by my parents and the community in which I grew up. I thought that what my parents believed and what they taught me was gospel. We may not realize it, but some of the values we hold dear are not even *our* values; they are those of our parents, our communities, our religion, or even our friends or employers. So I advise you to take the time to think critically about what YOU value. Sometimes the reason people feel unfulfilled and unhappy in the workplace is because they think that they are acting on what they hold dear; but in reality, they are living according to someone else's values and expectations. They just don't realize it.

I grew up in a house where neither of my parents worked in corporate America. My mom was a teacher and my dad worked for city government. I grew up believing that corporate America was based on greed and that people who worked for large corporations only valued money. I was raised to believe that if I wanted to contribute to society I needed to find a home in education (which is where I started my career) or "helping people" by working for the government. So, following college graduation I worked for one of the local colleges while I pursued a master's in education with the idea that I would become a school guidance counselor and coach basketball. Within a year, I realized that advancement where I worked wasn't necessarily based on outperforming your peers; instead, it was based on tenure and advanced degrees.

I looked around and saw that many of the people I respected, and who had been working at the college for years, were not living the lifestyle I wanted. I didn't consider myself greedy, but I did have a vision for how I wanted to raise my kids, where I'd like to live, and the car (or truck) I'd like to drive. For the first time I questioned what my core values really were and I assessed my priorities and expectations. After some serious reflection, I decided that I should look at career opportunities outside my comfort zone.

I've always been a hard worker, unafraid of challenging myself. I wanted to find a place that valued hard work and paid for performance, not degrees or tenure.

As it happened, one of the women I worked with had a son who worked for a local staffing company. She thought I would make a great recruiter or salesperson and she recommended I talk with her son. I jumped at the opportunity. As excited as I was to explore something new, I still had some trepidation that my parents would be disappointed in my decision. However, my parents, being the supportive people they've always been, were very happy for me. For the first time in my adult career, I began to earn pay commensurate with my level of work and effort. I found that to be very motivating and energizing. As the years progressed, my values, priorities, and expectations evolved, as did my career. But I could find what I needed at every stage in the industry I chose.

It takes courage to let go of your old beliefs and values. It can be scary, especially if these are values that were a part of your identity and you're afraid of disappointing people. Sometimes your values change because they have been linked to a former version of yourself. Perhaps when you started out you valued making a lot of money, hustling, and getting to the C-suite. But after years of grinding, your values have shifted and that lifestyle no longer aligns with the direction you want to take your life. Maybe you want to try something new and explore new career options. It's okay to admit that you want different things as you age and grow. But you must be willing to let go of your former identity as well.

Just a brief caution: It's a slippery slope. I have heard many people say that they aren't going after a job because it goes "against their core values" and who use that as an excuse to remain comfortable rather than trying something new. That's okay, too, but it's important to acknowledge that it's not a path to growth or self-actualization.

The key is to be consistent and serious when aligning your values, priorities, and expectations with your career path. This keeps you from taking jobs out of desperation. When you are clear about what you're looking for in a career, you can be clear to bosses or potential employers and are more likely to find a job that suits you.

Your value as a human being is inherent. You matter and your work matters. Just because an employer doesn't see that, or you don't have the freedom to work according to your values, doesn't mean you should make concessions. It just means you need to try different avenues to get to the right place for you. One way to do that is to begin to build a record of excellence in the areas of work you value most.

Exercise: Determining Your Values

While your values may be very clear to you and may be easy to articulate, some people have trouble identifying what matters most to them. They might have been doing what others wanted for so long that they've lost sight of what they care about.

Candace once asked an attorney who had come to her for coaching a simple question: "What kind of work would make you happy?" To her astonishment, the woman burst into huge, gasping sobs. She'd never given herself permission to use the words "work" and "happy" in the same sentence, which explained why she was so miserable at her firm, despite being a top earner. She had no idea of how to begin to think differently about her career. (Candace says, "So much for believing there's no crying in career coaching. I started keeping a box of tissues on hand at all times.")

So here's an exercise to help you get in touch with your priorities.

Start by finding a quiet spot to think about your "ideal" day on the job. Don't worry about the work you've done before, or what jobs you think might be available, focus on now.

Take a moment here to describe your perfect day at work:

1. What are you doing?

2. What makes the work worthwhile?

3. Are you working alone or with a team?

4. If you are working with a team, are you leading the team?

5. What kind of work are you doing? Is it:

    ◦ Creative work like marketing or working in the arts?

    ◦ Communicating, in writing or by public speaking?

    ◦ Solving tough problems based on evidence?

○ Making, repairing, or building things?

○ Performing detailed administrative work?

○ Helping customers, patients, or people find solutions or live better lives?

○ Directly providing vital services (like healthcare or counseling)?

○ Providing personal services (like beauty, hair, cooking, massage)?

○ Working outdoors, with plants or with animals?

○ Providing public safety?

Once you've pictured your ideal work and working conditions, think about what your activities are, the environment you work in, and how the people you work with make you feel. Those emotions help identify and label your values.

Here are some examples of emotions and ideals that identify values:

• Pride in your work/accomplishment

• Creating policies that make the company a better place (HR) or that make the community a better place (government)

• Knowing that you're helping people/animals/the environment

• Creating order from chaos/getting the right answer out of complex data

• Making your community safer

• Being or becoming a strong leader

• Being well-compensated for the work you do

• Winning awards/recognition/business/being considered the best at what you do

BUILD A RECORD OF EXCELLENCE

In the gap between where we are and where we
want to be lies our greatest opportunity for growth.

—**Dan Sullivan and Ben Hardy,**
The Gap and the Gain

At CSI, we encourage our employees to think of themselves as entrepreneurs. Our culture reflects a belief that employees, no matter what their role, should always seek out opportunities for growth. I love it when an employee alerts me to an area or issue I never thought of or when they anticipate trends, identify gaps in our processes or services, and find ways to address them. What separates the merely competent employees from the truly excellent comes down to having a growth mindset. We've covered this already in a previous chapter, but it bears repeating—the precursor for excellence is curiosity. But it doesn't stop there. It is what you *do* with that curiosity that ultimately counts.

Tessa White, CEO of The Job Doctor and author of the book *The Unspoken Truths for Career Success*, suggests that employees should always be on the lookout for opportunities in what she calls "the gap." In other words, what sets an employee apart—and adds relevance—is when an employee can see what's missing or not working long before they're asked to see it.[1]

White argues that most employees see their job descriptions as "gospel" and that deviating from these descriptions, let alone anticipating growth opportunities, is a cardinal sin. This, she says, is what is holding employees and companies back from achieving their goals. In my experience, the job description is a loose outline of what is required. While it's important and necessary as a guideline for what an employee *must* achieve, it often doesn't fully reflect the potential of the role—or what a person in that role *can* achieve.[2]

Most of us in recruitment realize that a job description is more like a set of guardrails designed to steer you in the general direction, and less like a specific GPS route to getting there. In the end, you are the driver and the person deciding where to go and what roads to take. Job descriptions are by no means comprehensive. If you have ever found yourself arguing with a manager and saying, "But I did everything in my job description—and I'm still not getting ahead," then you'll want to pay close attention to this section.

If you aspire to be in the driver's seat of your career, you'll need to prove your excellence. There are several ways to do that: show initiative, get creative about how you approach your job, or find the gaps and work hard to fill them.

> "It is not the strongest of the species that survive, not the most intelligent, but the one most responsive to change."
>
> **—Charles Darwin**

GAPS CAUSED BY TRENDS
OR SHIFTS IN YOUR INDUSTRY

Recently, a friend shared how her architect husband Greg took back the wheel of his career in the early 2000s in a way that is literally paying dividends today. Though Greg is now a majority partner in his firm, he started as a young, unlicensed architect working to accumulate the required hours to sit for his licensure exams. One day after work, he read an article about the need for LEED (Leadership in Energy and Environmental Design)-certified architects in the growing green-building economy. Though he didn't have his official architect's license, he realized he didn't need it to become LEED-certified. All he had to do was study for the exam and pass it.

However, the "all he had to do" part was quite difficult. At the time, he had a six-year-old and a newborn; he had just moved into a DIY fixer-upper and had very little bandwidth at the end of long days in the office. Nevertheless, he committed to studying every night for several months and took the test. Then he walked into his office and showed the managing partner what he had done—he had passed the exam and the company now had a LEED-certified architect who knew how to submit all the necessary forms for government and commercial contracts on behalf of the company.

This floored the managing partner, for whom LEED certification was a new concept. It opened an entirely new line of business—and a burgeoning one at that. No one asked Greg to do this, but it saved his career, and the firm, when things changed dramatically. Within a couple of years, the housing market and economy had crashed, and his firm was forced to lay off several architects. But because Greg was the only LEED-certified architect who could manage their government projects (which happened to be the only work that wasn't stalled by the housing crash), he was safe.

Greg eventually took all the necessary architecture licensure tests as well, and when it came time to select a new partner, the managing partner remembered Greg's initiative. Greg was chosen as the new partner.

What Greg did was anticipate a gap. He saw that the world was moving toward LEED-certified buildings and his company didn't have a LEED-certified official, which was required for all LEED contracts. He paid attention to trends in his industry and was able to get ahead of this one by learning about this particular niche, then doing what it took to follow through. While it certainly helped him and his career, the move also was a great service to the organization.

Greg's story is just one example, and it is replicable in any industry. Every industry has trends—and newsletters and blogs dedicated to discussing those trends. The daily news constantly alerts us to needs and gaps. One of the best ways to anticipate the needs within your organization's industry is to look outside what your organization is doing—and find out what others are doing (and doing well). Now, I am not saying every idea will have value or can be implemented. But most leaders will not balk at an employee who takes the initiative and thinks ahead—not just for themselves but for the entire organization.

> "Success is nothing more than a few simple
> disciplines, practiced every day."
>
> **—Jim Rohn**

GAPS WITHIN SKILLSETS

You don't necessarily have to anticipate future trends to fill a gap. Sometimes there are current areas within an organization that have "gaps." Maybe someone hasn't ever thought of streamlining a complicated process or maybe there is just "no time" to do what needs to be done. Sometimes the gap is a "skills gap." For example, if you work in the nonprofit world and develop the skills to become an excellent grant writer, you'll be relevant wherever you go. Grant writing is a skill that every nonprofit needs. But it's also a skill that when implemented can serve and help the entire organization, not to mention the cause you're raising funds or awareness for.

While it's absolutely imperative to stay up-to-date with current and new technologies, an often-overlooked way of proving excellence is to become proficient in the technology and applications already available to you. Is there a new app or program that you could become the resident expert in? Or are you skilled in a program no one else is and can train others to use it?

Every decade or so, a new technology emerges to change the way we do business (in the late 1980s and early 1990s it was email, later in the '90s, the internet, the 2000s brought the smartphone and apps, and now we have AI). And every new technology presents several challenges to remain relevant:

First, you have to understand the technology, learn its capabilities and how it will improve your productivity.

Second, you'll need to learn how to use it through training or experimentation.

That's the baseline for staying relevant, but it's still just reactionary. To become indispensable, you'll need to master using the technology. (Bonus points for becoming an early adopter, recommending it to your team, and helping them learn its features.) It's hard work, and not for the faint of heart, because sometimes that technology is coming for your job.

As I write this, Artificial Intelligence (AI) is the killer app that everyone is worried about. According to an online article by Lauren Comander for Florida International University's School of Business, "A poll by Morning Consult shows that two out of every three American adults worry about AI-driven job losses across industries. ChatGPT itself predicts that it will replace 4.8 million jobs."[3]

Already, generative AI is being used to create web copy, write newspaper articles and legal briefs (and innumerable high school and college essays and homework assignments), generate product descriptions, and generally take over thousands of tasks humans spend time on.

The idea that an algorithm could do in a few seconds the work that takes you hours is a scary thought. And while many journalists, writers, administrators, artists, and marketers are at home hiding under the covers, a few are embracing this new technology. They're the ones who will be relevant five years from now.

One of those embracing AI is Jennifer Chapman, vice chair of client relationships at Mayo Clinic in Jacksonville, Florida. Candace has known Jennifer for years and was intrigued when she noticed Jennifer's LinkedIn post about passing an online AI certification course for marketers.

In their conversation, Candace learned that Jennifer's employer has strict guidelines around the use of AI (clinical or patient information is strictly prohibited; employees don't even use "Mayo Clinic" in queries or prompts. They enter "Large healthcare system" or other generalized information.) But Mayo Clinic encouraged their staff to learn more about AI technology to use it effectively and ethically. So, Jennifer took the Ragan Communications six-hour online course, designed for communicators to help "galvanize everything from content creation to audience engagement."[4]

Jennifer says she uses AI not to generate content, but to help her be more productive and efficient with her content. For example, she can use AI to create an outline for a presentation or generate a script for a slide deck in seconds. She uses it to create thank-you notes after interviews and partner meetings. "I create a prompt that includes specifics of the meeting, and AI turns out a professional and thoughtful thank you," she says. "I can quickly check it over for accuracy and [my] voice and send it off in an email."

She also uses AI to generate ideas for articles (but not write them) and to check her writing for clarity and for audience appropriateness. AI gives her feedback on whether her writing should be more technical (or less) and checks for hidden bias in her approach or language. "I use AI as a bookend tool," she says. "It helps with ideas at the beginning of a project and with feedback at the end of it."

Jennifer's convinced that the professionals who will remain relevant through the AI era are those who learn how to craft the right prompts to get results. She says it's the most revolutionary productivity tool in history, taking on routine tasks that currently eat dozens of human hours every week. Transcribing notes from meetings or training sessions, updating policies or job descriptions, or writing routine correspondence can be done in a fraction of the time it takes now.

"But it's always going to need a human at the center of the work," she says.

Perhaps there are gaps in training tools. A worker in Candace's organization once admitted that she really struggled when she was hired because there was no guidebook for her. She wished she had an easy checklist that described her duties. Eventually she said, "Everybody's struggling with the same questions. I'm struggling with the same processes! What if I created a simple checklist or wrote a script to help people do it better?" She had not only asked the right question, but she also went on to take the initiative and create the guidebook. She even began coaching and training her peers. What was once complicated and obtuse became much more manageable. The result? New employees got more productive more quickly. Employee retention improved. And retention means that the organization's smartest workers stayed and strengthened the overall performance.

"Ideas are easy. Execution is everything."

—John Doerr

CREATE VALUE: DO YOUR RESEARCH
AND BE READY TO EXECUTE.

A word of caution, however: Nobody likes a know-it-all who comes in as a new hire full of suggestions and ways to "do it better." We have all had those experiences when a new person arrives—someone with zero experience or background—who begins firing off complaints about processes and offering unsolicited advice. Cue the eyerolls and the "Why didn't we think of that?" comments.

The best new hires are those who master their basic job skills and become competent before they seek to improve the system. They listen more than they talk, and they become very good at what they do within the current system. Along the way, they note what seems more complicated or less effective than it could be, along with ideas for improvement. No less a rule breaker than Pablo Picasso is famously attributed as having said, "Learn the rules like a pro, so you can break them like an artist."

Again, curiosity is key. Before you make assumptions or offer suggestions, do your research. Find out if someone has done the work or already tried to do things differently. And before you complain, be prepared to do something about it. It's worth repeating: The key to being able to improve processes is to first understand and be very competent at the job *you have now*. Do your job well. Earn the respect of your team. Be taken seriously. Then you will be encouraged to offer suggestions, changes, or to fill in a gap, especially if the process or suggestion has a positive impact on the bottom line of the company and creates value. For example, Greg couldn't have become a LEED-certified architect without being good at the job he did have. Going the extra mile implies you have walked a few miles already.

One of my favorite stories of an employee who created real value happened right here at CSI. We often run very large IT projects, working with hospitals that are converting to Electronic Health Records (EHRs). As they're converting, there's all kinds of tracking that needs to go on—who is assigned to what part of the hospital, for example—with lots of different variables. One of our biggest issues has always been dealing with complexity: How do you schedule hundreds of people with multiple shifts in multiple locations? It's a logistics nightmare. Imagine, a thousand people flying into a city for three or four weeks to help a healthcare system go live. They need plane reservations, accommodations, local travel, and meals. How does one track all that?

At the time, there wasn't a system available that could manage it all. Over the course of several years, a manual process evolved that included basic software and lots of Excel spreadsheets. (And lots and lots and lots of long nights and expensive man hours.) We attempted to hire consultants to build a software system and were repeatedly told it was all but impossible to try and develop something this complex.

Then one of our IT leads went out in the field and watched the process at several different client sites. After conducting a considerable amount of research, she felt confident her team could develop software in-house to manage the process. Everyone was skeptical. She hired a couple of developers and, though it took six months, they developed an entire system that not only tracked the shift work but also tracked the hours for our payroll system. It includes features like geofencing, so we can use GPS to track where people are and make sure they're going to the right location. While everyone was naysaying ("No, this can't be done" and "It's too complicated"), our IT lead did the research and figured it out. Her curiosity and commitment to execute, not to mention a can-do positive attitude, transformed this process.

Not only was it beneficial to the company, but we now have clients who have seen it in action and want to buy the software from us. And as a bonus, it's become a huge licensing opportunity—creating a new revenue stream for CSI. The IT lead is proof that one employee doing her job exceptionally well can create huge value for an organization.

And I can guarantee she is an employee who will remain relevant forever—not just to me, but to everyone who works with her.

> "Start where you are. Use what you have.
> Do what you can."
>
> —Arthur Ashe

LET ME TAKE THIS OFF YOUR PLATE: SMALL EFFORTS THAT GO A LONG WAY.

While the IT lead's story is extraordinary and a wonderful example, not every suggestion or process improvement will be a game-changer for an organization. Fortunately, there are plenty of ways you can make an impact in your organization at every level, especially if you're new and have yet to prove yourself.

Candace once described her marketing career as "a mixed bag of fun and not fun stuff." She wasn't interested in data mining social media or parsing the return on Google Ads; strategy was where she excelled. "Create the right messages, and you'll connect with your audience," she says. But analytics is how an organization measures results. Luckily, Joy, her right-hand person, loved it. "She had worked in a technical role before, and so she happily dove headfirst into data. She read my strengths—and weakness—and she figured out the gap. She taught herself the latest trends through online courses and by following experts and became an invaluable part of the team. She gained the confidence and the respect of the IT staff because she was the go-to resource for online analytics."

Joy approached taking on a new role with exactly the right touch:

"Let me take this off your plate, Candace. Let me help you with this so you can focus on other things." Joy realized Candace was busy, and she used this as an opportunity to showcase her skills by helping. You can do this too, wherever you are now.

Think of your role right now and your relationship with your other teammates or boss. Is there anything you see that isn't being done because of their lack of interest, skills, or time? Is there something you wish you could be doing and think you might be good at?

The formula we just offered is the perfect, non-threatening, "I'm not trying to take your job away" method to approach a leader or peer. "Here, let me take (insert the name of the task) off your plate. I really enjoy this work and I think I can do it well." Very few people will refuse such an offer. If you're currently unemployed and looking for work, is there a business where you can offer your services as a temporary side hustle? Can you say, "I'm really great at X, and I'd be happy to help take that off your plate"?

Demonstrating excellence isn't only about showcasing your abilities or strengths, it's also highlighting other team members, training or motivating others, or being an invaluable and supportive team member. Performing small, generous acts of support on a daily basis goes a long way. Never underestimate how refreshing a positive, helpful, and can-do person on a team can be. When everyone is down or feeling stressed, you can offer an encouraging word or help others see beyond their own work or limitations—and you will stand out.

But let's not forget our friend Brooke from the Introduction, who was taking on tasks that didn't add to her professional reputation. If you offer to help, help with something that shows off your professional abilities, rather than making you look like the office mom. Candace recalls a day when she was preparing to welcome her new administrative assistant.

Candace's love language is acts of service, so she'd just finished stocking her admin's new desk with office supplies and was getting ready to clean and disinfect the desk surface. One of her staff came and gently took the cloth out of her hand and did the cleaning himself. "No," he said firmly. "Vice presidents don't do office housekeeping." He was serious—and thoughtful—and she took his advice seriously.

"All progress takes place outside the comfort zone."

—Michael John Bobak

PUSHING PAST YOUR OWN LIMITS

Part of building a record of excellence and standing out requires you to push yourself beyond your comfort zone and self-imposed limitations. It's imperative that you get comfortable being uncomfortable. It's also not a bad idea to step out of your cubicle or away from your desk and look at what's going on around you. You may find you've outgrown the place, or perhaps it's the opposite; maybe things are changing fast, and you might not have a job in a few years. Economies, markets, and organizations shift all the time, and if you're not taking the temperature of your company's viability and your place in it, you're missing key opportunities for growth. Worse than that, if you get too comfortable, stay too long, or bury your head in the sand, you may not see that things have already changed. In fact, you may find yourself out of a job or that you have missed the optimal moment to pivot your career.

Often, people so strongly identify with a job or a role that it's difficult for them to imagine doing anything else. When we limit what we believe we can do, we limit our perception. For example, we once had a salesperson who refused to call on a major health coverage provider in our region because he believed "there was no business there." He had called the company a few times in the past and had no luck. So he gave up. When a new salesperson called on the company, he landed a sizable deal. Perhaps there was a new person at the company calling the shots. Perhaps the new salesperson tried a different strategy the previous one hadn't considered. Perhaps the landscape or competition changed. I am not sure. The point is this new salesperson didn't limit himself. He didn't say, "I can't do that, because the previous salesperson couldn't do it." He put himself out there and tried.

Many of us let other people's choices, decisions, or results limit our own. But sometimes we limit ourselves by the decisions we made long ago. George Lucas is widely credited as having said, "We are all living in cages with the door wide open." We unwittingly box ourselves into a career or a job, not realizing that we may have outgrown it or desire something new. I love it when employees come to me and say, "I love it here! I love this company and I want to be successful and be of service. But I don't necessarily love what I am doing now. Is there anything else I could try? And what do I need to learn to build a bridge to that path?" When employees are open to learning a new job and entering a new career path, it tells me they don't simply have a "job" mentality—they are actively looking for ways to stay engaged and curious.

When someone has what I call the "ownership" mentality, they look at their job and their career as something they own and control. They feel engaged and committed to the value they add to a company. They come into work each day with a feeling of pride. They want their company to succeed, and they want to play a role in that success. Excellent employees are always looking for ways to add value.

Exercise: Ways to Start Building a Bridge

Start where you are: Read the following exercises and choose one (or more) to try this week.

Hire a coach or find a mentor. Not everyone can afford to hire a career coach, but a coach can be invaluable in helping identify your strengths while also being honest with you about areas where you need to improve. If you can't afford a coach, consider reaching out to a trusted confidant, coworker, or a mentor who can offer an objective viewpoint. If you're a former student, remember that many colleges also have Career Resource Centers for their alumni with coaching and career advice.

Coaching resources at Better Up can help connect you with an online career coach. LinkedIn.com is another great place to search for a local coach. Just enter "career coach" or "executive coach" in the search engine and LinkedIn will return a list of profiles that might be a match. If you're not sure how to select the right coach, Google can help. An online search for "how to find the right career coach" turns up plenty of useful articles.

Join a professional organization with ongoing learning and networking opportunities. There are professional organizations for every job level, career, and industry. Google your industry, career, or profession and find a network to join. Attend their meetings and conferences and gather information about upcoming trends in your field. Every city has a Chamber of Commerce, and most offer leadership bootcamps, workshops and seminars, and networking events. You will not only meet people within your industry but those outside it as well. Your local Business Journal (most major cities have one) will frequently host events and lunch and learns.

Subscribe to newsletters, blogs, and LinkedIn Groups in your desired industry. There is no shortage of newsletters, blogs, and online career groups. Select a few that resonate with you and engage with them—subscribe to them, read them, comment, connect through the comments, share your own insights. Be willing to learn as well as share what you know. Again, this is an area where you can build your knowledge, collect new ideas, and meet other people in an online community while learning new perspectives and best practices in your industry.

Read books and listen to podcasts by experts in your desired fields or industry. There are millions of books and podcasts on virtually every niche topic. You can always find anything you are interested in by searching "the best of X industry" or "most interesting X podcast." Select a few and do a deep dive. Become an expert in a niche that you are passionate about and that will bring value to any organization. Don't be afraid to share what you learn with others.

Take an online class or certification class (not necessarily a degree) at your local university. Thanks to websites like Udemy, Teachable, and MasterClass, you can take hundreds of classes at a very low cost. Even Ivy League schools like MIT and Harvard offer free courses online that anyone can enroll in. Most universities now also offer certificate programs—LEAN Certification, Executive Leadership, AI Masterclasses, Graphic Design, communication and business writing, coding, UIX, Design Thinking, Innovation, are just a few examples. If you're interested in a topic that might improve the bottom line of an organization, make the case for attendance to your manager—the company might even pay for it.

Do at least one thing every day (even if you're not being paid) that moves you closer to your career of choice. This can be as simple as reading a chapter in a book about the field you're studying. It could be networking for an hour with industry peers or talking to a mentor about your goals. It could look like writing an action plan, taking a new course, or studying for a licensing exam that will take your career to the next level. Maybe it's listening to a podcast on your way to work, writing for twenty minutes a day, or meeting with a career coach for an hour.

Get "meta" about your job and career. "Meta" means going beyond mastering job skills. There is "doing your job" and then there is meta—thinking about doing your job *better*. It's constantly examining your job and career and asking: How can I improve this? How can I get better? How can I get ahead and take control of my career?

It's diving deeper into a topic you're passionate about. For example, horror novelist Stephen King wrote a book called *On Writing* that is "part memoir, part master class by one of the bestselling authors of all time." In the book, King takes a practical view of writing and explores the various tools every writer must use. He writes about the act and the art of writing—how he does it, what motivates him, what inspires him, what his process is. Even if you're no Stephen King, becoming truly proficient at anything means that you could literally "write a book" about it because you know it so well.[5]

So ask yourself: What do you know so well, you could write about it or teach it to someone else? That is where your strength lies and where you can begin to build your record of excellence.

REFRAME YOUR STORY

Each problem has hidden in it an opportunity so
powerful that it literally dwarfs the problem. The
greatest success stories were created by people who
recognized a problem and turned it into an opportunity.

—**Joseph Sugarman,** American author

LIVING IN THE SOLUTION

At CSI we often talk about "living in the solution." It is a mantra here.
I love to tell my coworkers, "Don't just bring me problems, bring me
solutions." When someone lives in the solution, they don't just become
adept at identifying what's gone wrong, they see that only as step one—
because if there is a problem, there is also a way to solve it.

So many of us live in the problem instead. We talk endlessly about
what is going wrong—the traffic on the way to work, the weather, the
news, our health, what someone else said or did. It's so easy to get caught
up in the same old negative stories. If you recorded all your daily conversations, how many of them would be complaints? How many would
be solutions?

Candace worked for a nonprofit that helped mid-career job seekers who had been laid off or fired. A common refrain was "No one will hire me!" These people then went on to complain about the myriad of issues facing them—their health, their lack of income, their past job experiences, the current job market.

I am not downplaying or dismissing their problems. I know how difficult and stressful it is to be out of work and facing so much uncertainty. However, I have found that, without exception, people who keep beating the drum of their problems never march forward into a new career or better opportunities—the solutions. The more they cling to the narrative that they are unemployable, the more they manifest that reality.

The stories you tell yourself are self-fulfilling prophecies. You get what you believe to be true, and if you believe you are never going to find work, you won't.

The part of the work I found most frustrating was trying to convince others that how they spoke about themselves and what they believed to be their reality was what was holding them back. I have heard every reason in the book why someone couldn't find work:

> *I am too old.*
> *I am too young.*
> *I earned too much money.*
> *I have too much experience.*
> *I don't have the credentials.*
> *I am overqualified.*
> *I am underqualified.*
> *I am X race, religion, gender, sex.*
> *I am not good at technology, but I am good with people.*
> *I am only good at tech stuff. I am not a people person.*

I am an old dog and can't be taught.
I am not good looking or current on fashion. (Sometimes said with
resignation, sometimes with a bit of pride.)

The more we cling to "I am" statements—or identity-based state-ments—the less flexible we become and the more likely we are to dig our heels in the sand. Often to our own detriment.

Several years ago, Candace was searching to hire someone in a front-facing PR position. This person had to be ready to handle press inquiries on camera at a moment's notice. Jacksonville, Florida, is a mid-size market with over one million residents in ten counties who pay attention to the regional news. On any given day, journalists from a local news station might call and say, "We're doing a story on summer employment for interns (or other timely employment topic or career advice). We can be there for an interview in ten minutes."

One job candidate showed up to interview for the PR job wear-ing a worn sweater, scuffed casual shoes, and wrinkled pants. She wore no make-up and hadn't bothered to comb her hair. While her resume was excellent, this appearance told us she didn't care enough how she appeared to others. With one glance, it would be easy to dismiss her and not take her seriously. It was obvious that those on the interview committee had eliminated her as a candidate as soon as she walked into the room.

To be fair, she'd spent most of her career in a small town outside metro Jacksonville where most broadcast stations wouldn't require her to travel much. She'd also worked in PR in a field unrelated to the one she was now applying for. It's one thing to have a long learning curve ahead; but no one wants to worry every day about whether this candi-date presented—or even cared about—embodying the right image.

Candace felt for her. She approached the woman after the interview and asked if she would be willing to hear some candid feedback on how the interview went. The candidate agreed. Candace then asked if she would be open to changing her appearance and her wardrobe on a regular basis, as this job would require her to be camera ready—and appearances matter in the media. The board wanted someone who looked trustworthy, polished, and authoritative, someone who looked like they paid attention to the details. The candidate immediately grew defensive.

"This is who I am," she countered. "And it's worked for me for years. I don't think how I dress or look should matter. The only thing that matters is whether I can say the right things about what the organization does."

Candace nodded and didn't press further. "You're right—everybody should be comfortable in who they are. Thank you so much for sharing that." She thanked her for coming, but Candace knew that others on the hiring committee would rule her out. And sure enough, the PR candidate was not considered for a second interview.

The story this candidate told herself is: "I am fine the way I am; the world is what needs to change." While that may be true—everyone has a right to be who they are—how you present yourself is how you present the company. A professional appearance instills trust in both. It's important to realize that certain positions have certain requirements. An on-air news journalist is expected to dress professionally, with their hair styled and any make-up well done. Those who work in restaurants are expected to come to work showered and clean as their appearance (especially the host) sets the tone for the entire experience. Have you ever dined at a restaurant where the waiter wore a dirty apron or a stained shirt? How likely would you be to eat at a place where the server's hands looked unclean or their hair was uncombed or messy? Whether we acknowledge it or not, appearances do matter.

We will get into how to make those external changes in the next chapter, but in this section we'll go deeper into adjusting the internal mindset and stories that hold you back from starting those necessary changes.

There will always be guidelines for every role. You can either spend your time arguing against them and telling yourself a story about why you don't need to change, or you can do some digging, investigate, and get curious about what you need to do to adapt. To achieve your career goals, you might need to reframe your self-perception and the stories you've been telling yourself. Because if you change your story, you can change your life.

WHAT IS THE STORY YOU ARE TELLING?

The stories you repeatedly tell yourself and others communicate your perception of the world. Whether you are conscious of it or not, the choices you make every day—at work and home—are a direct reflection of the stories you carry around within you.

If you want a different outcome at work or in your career, you need to start telling yourself a new story. The best way to do that is to "reframe" your story. Now, reframing is not lying or masking the true parts; it's simply presenting or exploring a different perspective of who you are. It's modifying a narrative to tell a different story, and in doing so you reclaim a part of yourself. You may even discover parts of your life or career story that you had forgotten or neglected to share because it didn't fit the narrative you were used to telling.

FOCUSING ON THE "UNSTORIED"

There is such a thing as "Narrative Therapy," in which we can heal or reclaim our lives simply by telling different stories. According to authors and psychologists Gene Combs and Jill Freedman, in their book

Narrative Therapy: The Social Construction of Preferred Realities, "In any life there are always more events that don't get 'storied' than there are ones that do—even the longest and most complex autobiography leaves out more than it includes. This means that when life narratives carry hurtful meanings or seem to offer only unpleasant choices, they can be changed by highlighting different, previously un-storied events or by taking new meaning from already storied events, thereby constructing new narratives."[1]

Perhaps you keep repeating a story where "every" manager you ever had was a micromanager. Ask yourself: What parts are you leaving out of that story? Next, notice that word, "every." Words like "always," "never," or "every" are terms of absolutes; they indicate a tendency to overlook situations that prove to be the exception to the rule. Now, when you take these absolute words out of the sentence, what aspects of the story have you neglected to tell? Did you ever have a boss who encouraged you? Or who pointed out your mistakes in a constructive manner that helped? Are there any aspects of your behavior or personality that you neglected in the retelling? Maybe the person who seemed to be micromanaging you did so because of something you were or weren't doing? Be as objective as possible about your story. Maybe that "micromanaging" was simply more follow up than you were used to. Maybe it was just different from the way you prefer to follow up or oversee a project.

Sometimes two things can be true at the same time; a boss can be a micromanager, but genuinely kind and invested in her role. Can you look at someone and see both their negative and positive aspects? Can you do the same for yourself?

This is the first step in "reframing" your story. To revise the story you have been telling yourself, start by looking at the whole story, not just the parts that seem to fit your narrative of events.

THE ILLUSION OF NO CHOICE

The next step is to consider whether you have cast yourself as the "victim" or the "hero" of the story. Most people are a mixture of both throughout life; rarely are you one or the other. Sometimes, we're simply a member of the chorus—the story wasn't even about us, no matter how central we felt. Can you take yourself out of either role or cast yourself as simply a person who is learning life's lessons, rather than the person who is always the victim of some out-of-control situation? When you cast yourself as a "victim" you are powerless. Is that true? Are you powerless?

When we feel powerless, we believe we have no choice. But we *do* have a choice. We may not have a choice in whether we are fired, laid off, or whether our industry dramatically shifts, but we do have a choice in how we respond. Consider the story of two people arguing over whether a glass is half full (the "optimist") or half empty (the "pessimist"). While they are busy arguing, someone else grabs the drink and says he is the "opportunist." Reframing your story is a bit like that: rather than looking at a situation and seeing black or white, good or bad, positive or negative, looking at your stories with shades of gray, neutrally, or through lessons learned. This gives you a broader perspective. When you are in an impossible situation in which you have no control, it's sometimes helpful to look for what you can control. Look at any situation you are dealing with right now. What is in your power to change? Sometimes the only thing you have control over is where you choose to look.

There is a cute cartoon making its way around the internet that shows two men sitting on a train as it winds up a mountain. One man has turned his head so that he is staring at the wall of the mountain; as a result, he thinks the ride is terrible. The other man has his head turned toward the window; he is awestruck by his view of the world, the sunset, the mountains and valleys outside. How you choose to see the world truly depends on where you focus your attention.

ADJUSTING YOUR ELEVATOR SPEECH

Most of us have a story prepared when talking to people about what we do or the position we have. When someone asks you about your profession, what do you typically say? How do you talk about your life and your work? Most of us don't sit down and tell our entire life story from birth to the present day; we give an abbreviated version. We say where we are from, what we do, where we work. It's important to investigate what stories we tell and why. Another thing to inventory are the beliefs you hold dear. Or how you describe yourself. Sometimes we reduce ourselves to one word: Optimist. Realist. Liberal. Conservative. Family guy. Straight shooter. Servant leader. Perfectionist. Investigate why you do this. Where or from whom did these descriptions come? Do they accurately convey who you are? What is the story you put out in the world? Are there some statements you hear yourself saying repeatedly? Is there an underlying theme?

Here are some examples:

> *No matter what I do, nothing works out.*
> *Everything always works out for me.*
> *There are good days and bad days, and I just go with the flow.*
> *Nothing lasts forever. I don't ever get too comfortable.*
> *I am not a people person.*
> *I don't do crowds.*
> *I love people.*
> *I can do just about anything I set my mind to.*
> *I had a terrible childhood and suffered a lot of abuse; this is why I don't trust people.*
> *I had a terrible childhood, but I have come a long way, and I am proud of my journey to wholeness.*
> *I'm a survivor.*
> *I have the worst luck.*
> *I am so blessed and lucky.*
> *I am so grateful for the tough times; they really taught me how to be a better person.*
> *Without X (my family, my health, my career, my whatever), I'm nothing.*

WHERE THE BELIEFS AND STORIES COME FROM

Most of the stories we tell ourselves are reinforced by our families. According to psychotherapist and writer Kaytee Gillis, LCSW-BACS, most dysfunctional families unknowingly cast their kids at an early age in roles such as the golden child, hero, rebel, black sheep, favorite, prodigal child, smart one, comedian, mascot, grump, drama queen, patient, enabler, or a parent/child (a child who assumes the role of parent to maintain control and safety), and many more.[2] If any of these sound familiar, if you have assigned these terms to other family members or they have been assigned to you, there's some comfort in knowing that this is normal. Most families do this, but it is a survival mechanism—not a life sentence. Our roles in life can and will change over time. Perhaps you have been unwittingly cast into multiple roles at the same time, or for a duration of time. But these stories and roles serve a purpose. "Casting" certain roles and assigning blame or accolades creates a sense of balance in what can be a chaotic and often indescribable experience. It also helps parents and siblings by letting them provide canned responses ("There she goes again") rather than being present in the moment and focusing on what's really happening.

Many families also have myths and stories they pass on from generation to generation, and few people question why family dynamics are the way they are or whether patterns can change. Like all myths, family myths help make sense out of the nonsensical. They serve a purpose for a time, but unfortunately, many people carry these assigned roles into adulthood and even their professional lives—long after they proved useful or helpful. What may have helped someone survive a difficult childhood or situation may not necessarily help someone thrive in adulthood.

For example, take an employee who is overly eager to please. They seem to have no backbone; they are always jumping up to offer someone their chair or get coffee, even if their role doesn't require them to do so. They may apologize profusely for the smallest error, even when they've done no wrong themselves. In their family, pleasing and apologizing may have spared them abuse or ridicule. So they grew up believing that to stay under the radar, they had to stay small. This is an old belief that no longer serves them. As a result, they're perceived as subservient and insecure, which makes other people believe they can never be a strong leader. Or they can't seem to get ahead in their work, and may even feel resentful for constantly being passed over for promotions even though, in their mind, they have "done everything right."

Most of us behave in the world in the manner we adopted at a very young age to survive. Perhaps you became a perfectionist as a child, because making the smallest error invited derision or admonishment. Today you sweat every detail and feel overwhelmed trying to make everything "perfect," so much so that you can't move forward, because you are so wrapped up in making your work just so.

We usually announce these outmoded ideas and beliefs we have adopted about ourselves in our "elevator speech"—the shorthand story of who we are or what we do.

Take a moment and think back to your past few interactions with people in which someone asked you about yourself or what you do. What did you tell them?

HOW DO YOU DEFINE YOURSELF?

How you define yourself matters. Sit in on any brand development meeting and you'll be asked to think of several words to describe the brand—usually these are adjectives that "sum up" the product or service, for example: customizable, adaptable, comprehensive, classic, established, innovative, knowledgeable, modern, luxurious, original, professional, sustainable. When people think of Chanel, they think of luxury, classic, or exclusive style. When people think of Nike, they are inspired ("Just do it" is their tagline) and think of elite and versatile athletic shoes/clothing.

In today's workplace, it's not just corporations or companies that have a brand; people do, too. You'll be encouraged to work on your "brand" or "image" in the final Mirrorset chapters, but before we do that, let's look at the words you (or others) use to describe yourself *now*. This can be a list of adjectives or identifiers that serve as a shorthand to who you are and what you value. Position these as "I am" statements:

> *I am an American.*
> *I am a Texan/Floridian/Californian.*
> *I am a Republican/Democrat/Independent.*
> *I am single/married/divorced/dating/widowed.*
> *I'm a proud mom/dad of . . .*
> *I am employed/I am unemployed.*
> *I am spiritual/not religious/Christian/Jewish/Muslim/Buddhist.*
> *I am cautious.*
> *I am a risktaker.*
> *I am brave.*
> *I am a nervous person.*
> *I am a morning person.*
> *I am a night person.*
> *I am a coffee drinker.*
> *I am a tea drinker.*
> *I am a dog lover.*
> *I am a cat lover.*
> *I am a reader.*
> *I'm an athlete.*
> *I am a sports fan of [football, basketball, baseball, or any specific team].*

Get the picture? There are so many ways we describe ourselves—where we live, what we do, what we believe, what we love, what we hate, what we vote for, how we think. Together they are supposed to tell a story about who or what we are. But these "I am" statements don't tell the *whole* story. Reducing ourselves to a few blanket statements (and assigning them to others) can cause division, contradiction, and misunderstandings. To tell a different story, you need to find new and broader definitions of yourself.

How we describe ourselves can change what we think and believe, and even who we surround ourselves with. For example, if we limit our definition of ourselves by how we vote or what faith we practice, we begin to see the world as "us" versus "them." This closes us off to connecting with, reaching out to, and seeing others more fully. It also limits our capacity to change.

We've shared stories of people who thought they weren't right for a position because they carried around a limiting belief about themselves. It was only when that belief was challenged that they were able to see that they were capable of doing the work.

The best way to prepare yourself for a massive shift in how you look at yourself and how others look at you is to recast yourself in the story of your life. If you want the world to see you differently, you have to change the way YOU see the world.

The best way to do that is to tell a new version of the story you want to live.

Exercise 1: Restorying Your Life

1. Go back over childhood and early adulthood and think of those critical incidents that had something to do with the issues that are in conflict now. Rather than go year by year over your entire life, list major milestones. You may find it easier to break up your life into chapters based on important events such as a parental divorce, a death in the family, changing schools, moving, a bad breakup. Look for common themes to determine if there's a pattern that may indicate the stories that no longer serve you. Looking closely at your childhood experiences is

key because it is during those early childhood years when you developed your beliefs about the world. You may be carrying around a lot of outdated beliefs.

I recall a time I interviewed an undergrad student who was working on her master's degree in civil engineering. When she came into my office, she said, "I am really worried I won't be hired because I am a woman."

"Whoa!" I said, "that's not realistic at all!" At the time, her being a woman in STEM (Science, Technology, Engineering, Math) was a huge asset. (Still is.) But for some reason, she believed it was a detriment. I asked her to reconsider and to start thinking that the opposite was true. What if she went into every interview thinking: *They're only looking to hire a woman for this role.* And that is what she did. She is now a partner at a large civil engineering firm and has had a wonderful career.

2. Now think about a negative thing that happened to you. Perhaps you were turned down for a promotion or were rejected by the school of your dreams. Was there *any* positive outcome? Did you end up going to a different school and finding your life partner? Or perhaps, you didn't land the job of your dreams, but then discovered an entirely new dream or possibility.

    Alternatively, think of something positive or good in your life right now. If you can trace the experience backward through time, you may find that what you have now came as a result of something not working out or going according to plan. Setbacks are usually the first step in a comeback and rejection is often a redirection.

3. Next, write a story that focuses on the best parts of your personality, beliefs, and outlook. Imagine the highest version of yourself—what does that look like? What are you doing? What

are you working on? What do you believe? How do you move through the world? Sometimes looking at the future and projecting the story you want to be telling in three, four, or five years' time is the first step in changing your life. Write this story in the present tense ("I am"), as though it is already a reality.

4. Once you create the story you want to tell, act like the person you want to become. How do you dress? What does your daily routine look like? Who do you talk to and spend time with? How do you engage with others? For example, if until now, you have always been quiet in meetings and you aren't assertive, how can you demonstrate you are more outgoing? If you tend to overexplain and talk too much, what would it look like to prevent that in the future?

Exercise 2: Reframing Your Current Story

The first step to reframing a current story that no longer serves you is to realize this: It's simply a story you're telling yourself. Start with "The story I'm telling myself today is . . ." which allows you to see this story as flexible, fungible, and changeable. You have the power to become the author instead of simply a character. History, after all, is at its essence, *a* story of what happened—not *the only* story of what happened.

Cognitive Behavioral Therapy (CBT), a form of psychological treatment that involves efforts to change thinking and behavioral patterns, can offer a way to take back your power and agency when faced with a story that no longer serves you.

The process looks like this:

• The Three Cs of CBT are "Catch it, Check it, Change it."

- Acknowledge that something bad/unpleasant is happening or has happened.

- CBT practitioners/therapists work with clients to recognize how negative thought patterns influence a person's feelings and behaviors.

- Clients ask themselves how their own feelings, behaviors, and actions might have contributed to what happened.

- They write down a list of unproductive thoughts and behaviors.

- Then they replace them with more productive behaviors. For example, "No one appreciates the work I do" can be replaced with "My constant complaining about how busy I am might be turning people off."

- Recognize that it may take time to replace your negative thoughts.

Even if your story is true (you were treated unfairly, no one appreciates your work, people think you're too old/young to be effective), you still have the power to act. Rumination, going over and over a thought in your mind, is never productive. Instead, allow yourself a few minutes each day to be sad or mad about it, then put those feelings aside. (You can revisit them later if you need to.)

Now, ask yourself:

- What am I going to do about it?

- What steps can I take to break the cycle or change the ending of this story?

Take Action

When you find yourself ruminating, overthinking, or stressing about the future, it can help to make an action plan. Writing down your intentions (or a plan you aim to execute) makes them more real, and helps you focus when you feel out of control. Even small actions can give you a sense of agency; they can change your story from one of passive victimhood to that of an active character on a hero's journey.

What can you do today?

- Review your resume and update it to include your training, skills, and accomplishments over the past year (or more, if it hasn't been updated in a while.)

- Write a list of the successful projects you've completed over the past year. Start with a professional list that will be useful during a performance review or internal interview. Then write a list of personal accomplishments to remind yourself that you are a successful person in all aspects of life.

- Write a letter to your future self. Congratulate future you on turning around your current situation, landing the promotion or job of your dreams, or building or repairing an important relationship. This is an uplifting way of changing your story.

- Connect with someone you haven't seen for a while. Share some positive stories about yourself (no one will enjoy a gripe session after a long absence). Better yet, prepare questions to ask the other person about their career and accomplishments. (Bonus points for connecting to thank them or let them know how their advice or assistance made a difference for you!)

- Tell your story to someone or listen to their story. One quote that helps me keep perspective is from journalist Regina Brett: "If we all threw our problems in a pile and saw everyone else's, we'd [certainly want to] grab ours back."[3] Sometimes, telling your story to someone else gives you a fresh perspective on what you might be able to do about it. A trusted friend or family member—one who's on your side but knows you well enough to call you out if you're in the wrong or seeing things from a distorted point of view—may also have advice that helps. A beginner's mindset can offer an original take on what's happening right now.

- Choose to help people whose stories touch your heart. Volunteering for others in need is a great way to increase your empathy and lift the emphasis off what's happening to you. It also provides a sense of accomplishment, pride, and identity. And the better you feel about yourself, the more likely you are to have a positive view of your life and future.

WEEK 8

SELF-AWARENESS ACTION PLAN

'Insight is the booby prize of therapy' is my favorite maxim of the trade, meaning that you can have all the insight in the world, but if you don't change when you're out in the world, the insight and the therapy is worthless. Insight allows you to ask yourself, "Is this something that's being done to me or am I doing it to myself?" The answer gives you choices, but it's up to you to make them.

— **Lori Gottlieb,** psychiatrist and author of
Maybe You Should Talk to Someone

O ver the past few weeks, I've tried to give you a master class in self-awareness. We began this section by stating in the introduction to Skillset that insight doesn't lead to changed behavior. There comes a time when you need to put together all the knowledge and information you have gained from your introspection and start implementing changes. You can't get different results by doing the same thing over and over.

In week five we identified your needs, values, and non-negotiables. In week six, we focused on the areas where you could push past your own limits, fill gaps in your skillsets, and create value. And last week, we focused on reframing the story you've been telling others about your life and your present career. You know what you need to do. You know your weaknesses, your strengths, and you know the story you WANT to tell.

Now it's time to walk the walk. Many people stumble here. It's uncomfortable. It may feel like you're in a movie—you're acting like someone you're not. *At least not yet.* But, in some ways, I am asking you to do just that. I am not specifically advocating "fake it till you make it," but I am asking you to step into your future self and start acting like the person you want to be. This often leads people to feel as though they are "imposters" or that they are not worthy or deserving of a current or desired role. They might feel like everyone else knows something they don't.

Here's a secret: *Everyone is trying to figure it out as they go along.* You're not the only one. In fact, most of the people I have met who suffer from imposter syndrome are incredible at their jobs. That self-doubt and need to review their work and check in on what others think keeps them on their toes. Maybe you could "reframe" imposter syndrome, too. Think of it as: *competent syndrome.* What if you told yourself that you are competent at what you do? What if your "syndrome" helped you become more aware of how your actions affect others and showed that you care deeply about the results? Most people who are quick to announce that they are "killing it at their jobs" or "can do anyone's job" usually have no clue what they're talking about. Meanwhile, all the people who come across my desk pronouncing they don't have "what it takes" are some of the hardest working, most intelligent, and competent people I know.

When the urge to doubt yourself arises, ask yourself this. Instead of "What if everyone finds out I have no idea what I am doing?" train your brain to say, "If not now, then when? If not me, then who?" These are the two questions you need to repeatedly ask yourself. Someone has to do your job! Why shouldn't it be you? And why shouldn't you be great at it?

Do you want to waste another year, two years, or three doing what you have always done, or do you want to make serious changes that the person three years from now will thank you for? It's not going to be easy. In fact, it's going to get downright uncomfortable. But stick with me because it will be worth it.

I must warn you: This is where most people stop. They would rather buy another self-help book, hoping the answer to what ails them lies within the pages. They'd rather do a deep dive into their past. They'd rather scratch open an old wound. I am not going to let you do that. This week, we are going all in. This is your action plan. If you're serious about making changes, and you want to be fully prepared for the final month where we focus on your Mirrorset skills (how you look and appear to others), you need to do the following steps. Unlike every other section where we waited until the end of the chapter to introduce exercises, I suggest having a notebook handy because you will be making lots of lists. This is where the rubber meets the road, and you have a lot to do.

1. BECOME THE OWNER OF YOU, INC.

Even if you are currently employed or looking for work, adopt the mindset that you are now an independent contractor. And as a small business owner, you are constantly looking to "serve" your clients (i.e., your employer, customers, and colleagues). What does this mean? It means you have to draft a document that states what the "services" are you offer to others. It's time to flip the script of your current or desired job description and rewrite it as if you are the owner of a company that offers this service. By adopting the owner/entrepreneur mindset and rewriting your job description, you will be empowered to uphold your commitments. Like an owner, you'll be constantly looking for opportunities to help you, your coworkers, or company flourish and grow. Start to look for ways—this week—where you can raise your hand and volunteer your services for greater visibility. This entire week, I want you to carry yourself and behave as if "this is who I am now." As President Harry Truman's sign on his desk declared: "The buck stops with me."

You are now the boss of you. You have no one to blame. No excuses.

2. CREATE A DETAILED VISUAL LIST OF DAILY THINGS TO DO.

Perhaps you've heard this maxim: "You can't measure what you don't track." Most of us are well-versed in personal dashboards, scorecards, calendars, or online planners. And most of us would be lost without the automatic reminders of all our daily meetings. There are plenty of companywide platforms that track daily tasks and to-dos—Asana, Slack, Teams, as well as various calendar tools. And yet, how many of us will still forget an upcoming meeting? How many of us have every intention of taking a walk or going to exercise class, but skip it when our day goes off the rails? Ever wonder how it is that you can write something in your calendar and still forget it or lose track of time? You're not alone. By outsourcing your planning and record keeping to phone apps on other sources, you're actually *less* likely to remember what you need to do. Why? Because when we rely on something external, such as our phones to remind us, we can go through the days unconscious of what we truly want to accomplish.

There is a way to hijack this phenomenon. And it's as simple as *handwriting* these daily goals and keeping them visible and handy throughout the day. Each morning this week, I want you to wake up and write in detail (this is key) each goal or task you plan to accomplish. Why? According to a recent study conducted by leadership author

Mark Murphy, vividly describing your goals in written form is strongly associated with goal success. According to the study, "people who very vividly described or pictured their goals are anywhere from 1.2 to 1.4 times more likely to successfully accomplish their goals" than people who don't.[1] Manually writing down and describing in detail what you want to happen helps on two levels:

- First, it helps you store the information where you can review and look at it, repeatedly reminding you of what you have to do.

- Second, it helps on a neurological level. When you write things down manually (and descriptively), you "encode" the message into your hippocampus where the brain forms, stores, and processes memory. It's also where your brain decides to store or throw out anything it is supposed to remember. The more detailed our descriptions, the more likely we are to remember them.

This is why most of the daily tasks and to-dos we track on calendars and tracking apps still seem to fall through the cracks. We're not taking the time to write down in detail what it is we need to do.

3. HONOR YOUR COMMITMENTS AND FIND AN ACCOUNTABILITY PARTNER.

This seems easy enough. Most of us would be quick to say, "Of course I honor my commitments!" But do you? Do you make a list of things to do, but not complete them? Do you promise to show up to work on time yet roll in five minutes late? Do you agree to work terms but figure out how to take shortcuts? Do you ever break your own commitments to yourself? Honoring your commitments, even the smallest and seemingly insignificant ones, can add up.

Creating habits helps. Do anything for several weeks, and it becomes routine. But, for something to become a habit, you need to do it consistently, and that's where an accountability partner comes in.

Let's say your goal is to walk every day. You're more likely to put on your sneakers and head outside if you arranged to meet a friend at a park because you don't want to let someone else down. Likewise, when we start trying to make major changes in how we conduct ourselves in the workplace or in life, it helps to let someone know what we're doing and why we're doing it. Find someone you trust, who you won't mind checking in with, and who you know will encourage you to be honest. This should not be a boss or a manager, but rather a peer, colleague, spouse, or partner. For example, if you're intentional and committed about speaking up in meetings, tell a friend about your goal. Call or text them before the meeting and let them know: "I intend to speak up in our team meeting and voice my concerns about X." We are much more likely to do something when we verbally commit to it in front of a friend. Afterward, circle back and tell them whether you were successful or not.

Perhaps you've been advised that your "dad jokes" or "office humor" is cringeworthy and not appreciated. Tell someone about your intention to change that habit and then report back to them daily or weekly as to whether you were successful or not. Perhaps you talk too much or tell long, meandering stories, and have decided you need to listen more and only share salient points. Consider who is around you all day that will be able to observe you and give you feedback as to whether you succeeded in your goal.

Whatever the issue you need to work on, you don't have to do it alone. And it doesn't have to be punitive—it can be fun! A friend's daughter was always apologizing, saying "I'm so sorry!" over the smallest infraction, and it was irritating all her coworkers. They started an I'm Sorry Jar. Every time she apologized for something unwarranted, she put a quarter in the I'm Sorry Jar. By the end of the week, she had enough money to take her friends out for lunch. The following week she took them out for coffee. By week three, there were no coins in the jar.

Your accountability partner will come in handy as we work on Mirrorset skills in the coming weeks. Look for someone you trust to call on, especially when it comes to how you look and present yourself.

4. BE AWARE OF YOUR TRIGGERS AND SELF-SABOTAGING BEHAVIORS.

As a coach, Candace observes that her clients don't intend to break their commitments. What usually happens is that they are "triggered" by an event that activates a deep insecurity, so they fall back into their old habit or comfort zone.

We all have moments of weakness, stress, or overwhelm, and find ourselves slipping on our commitments or promises to ourselves. Perhaps you head to the cookie jar or a bag of potato chips after a particularly rough day. Some people crack a beer or uncork a wine bottle. We want to "take the edge off" of all the feelings that arise in us. Sometimes shame, embarrassment, criticism, and the mistakes we make, especially at work, can cause incredibly uncomfortable feelings. Most of these triggers come from our place of deepest insecurity— usually formed in childhood. And each of us has our own unique way of responding to these negative feelings. We all have a go-to survival mechanism (or two, or three, etc.). Maybe you talk too much; another person might clam up and shut down. One person may respond to criticism by crying, while another might be instantly defensive and go on the attack.

You can't fix or address what you don't acknowledge. The first step is to recognize your triggers and become very familiar with what sets you off on the wrong foot. When do you notice a negative or self-sabotaging behavior? What preceded it? What were you doing or feeling? Then ask yourself, how did this self-sabotaging behavior help alleviate this feeling? No one does anything without some reward. Even if the behavior is negative, we "get something out of it," intentionally or not. Perhaps we feel temporarily numb or more in control (at least at the outset). But then the shame comes back over what we have done, and the cycle starts all over again.

By becoming aware of our triggers, we can plan to respond in a way that would better serve us. For example, if you tend to talk too much or too fast when you feel nervous about meeting new people, put a plan in place: Take a deep breath and long exhale before you begin to speak. You may even tell yourself, "I will only say one thing; then I will ask a question to invite more conversation." Take a minute to think about your usual triggers, and the ways you frequently respond.

5. THE THREE ISSUES TO MASTER

Another reason that people don't honor their commitments is due to the sheer volume of them! They have simply taken on too many goals, resolutions, or self-help projects. It's the same reason why people don't keep their New Year's resolutions—they went too hard, too soon, with too many. When you're trying to implement radical changes into your life, you have to prioritize and choose which one, two, or three will have the biggest impact. What are the three things you can pick to track (daily or weekly) and be accountable for that would improve your career and your life? By narrowing down the options and focusing on one issue at a time, one day at a time, you're more likely to succeed. And if you're having troubling narrowing down your options, call on your accountability partner.

THE WORK IS NEVER DONE.

For the past month, we focused on becoming more self-aware about the changes we need to make to be more relevant; but it's important to note that this work is ongoing rather than static. Just like the workplace, times change, trends change, and what is acceptable changes. You can't just say, "This is who I am," and remain unchanged—even if you're a better you than you were before. The workplace—and life—demands that we keep up and adapt. And one very important way we keep up is, like it or not, our appearance. In the final weeks ahead, we're going to take everything we have learned from our Mindset and Skillset practices and apply them to our Mirrorset Practices.

SKILLSET SELF-ASSESSMENT

Now that you've begun work on your skillset, and completed the assessments and exercises along the way, you should be ready to identify what you'd like to change and how you're going to work on it. Let's look at the progress you've made and what still needs work.

On a scale of 1 to 5, with 1 being the least true and 5 being the truest, how would you rate yourself after four weeks of deciding what you want, where you want to be, and which steps to take to get there?

I feel that I understand my needs, values, expectations, and non-negotiables.

1	2	3	4	5

For the record, let's briefly list them here.

Needs:

_____

_____

Values:

_____

_____

Expectations:

_____

_____

Non-negotiables:

_____

_____

How many of the above are being met in your current job?

☐ Most of the above

☐ A few (list them below)

☐ Not many

☐ My career is not aligned with my needs or values

If you need to make a change, rank your needs, values, expectations, and non-negotiables in order of importance to you in your next role (from most important to least important):

Most Important   Least Important

_____

_____

Which skills make you most valuable to an employer (in your current role or a future one)? List them here.

_____

_____

_____

_____

Now, rate your current company/role in terms of these values:

Performance—and therefore pay commensurate with that performance.

| 1 | 2 | 3 | 4 | 5 |

Appreciation—rewarding employees for efforts (sometimes monetary compensation, but also verbal or written recognition).

| 1 | 2 | 3 | 4 | 5 |

Opportunities for Advancement

| 1 | 2 | 3 | 4 | 5 |

Opportunities to Give Back

| 1 | 2 | 3 | 4 | 5 |

Culture

| 1 | 2 | 3 | 4 | 5 |

Diversity

| 1 | 2 | 3 | 4 | 5 |

I believe that my expectations are a good match for my current skills and potential contribution to my employer (or a future one).

| 1 | 2 | 3 | 4 | 5 |

I believe that I am reliable and trustworthy. My employer and team members can count on me to do what I say I will.

| 1 | 2 | 3 | 4 | 5 |

If you believe your employer or coworkers can count on you, but you don't feel as though they do, what actions can help them transform their perception?

_____

_____

My record of excellence includes these skills/accomplishments:

_____

_____

I would like to challenge myself to develop these skills:

_____

_____

My quick action plan to develop these skills (for example: I will learn a new software program related to my field, I'll take a course in Generative AI, I'll volunteer for a project at work and turn it in ahead of time, etc.):

_____

_____

MONTH THREE

Mirrorset Practices

It's not what you look at that matters,
it's what you see.

—Henry David Thoreau

W hat do people see when they look at you? Note: I didn't ask what you *think* they see—but what do they *actually see?* Typically, what we think people see is very different from what they do see or rather what their perception of you might be.

I am going to be straight with you: This topic is tricky. While not judging others by their appearance—race, nationality, gender, body size, type, or abilities—is a very good thing, we all recognize we live and operate in a world where there are certain codes of conduct, such as grooming and dress, that workplaces deem appropriate. Ignoring the impact of how you show up in the world could cost you jobs, promotions, raises, or at the very least, respect from colleagues.

Thankfully, we have come a long way from a discriminatory workplace (though we still have a long way to go). We're also far from the days when men arrived at the office in three-piece suits and women were relegated to skirts and heels. Since the COVID-19 pandemic, when "WFH" (work from home) became the norm, many companies have stopped even trying to enforce dress codes, so grateful are they to have people in the office. That being said, just because the rules have grown lax doesn't mean people don't judge or categorize us based on appearance and presentation.

Whether we want to admit it or not, we all "show" others who we are before we even open our mouths. How we walk, carry ourselves, style, and dress, tells people who we are and what we value, stand for, and care about.

To disregard or neglect how you appear and interact with others is a grave mistake. Part of being relevant assumes that you have a sense of what is current and trending, or at the very least, what is out of fashion or obsolete. That you have some sense of social etiquette and norms. In an increasingly diverse workplace it's more important than ever to stay abreast of what is happening around you—and that means how you appear, behave, speak, and work with others.

In this section, we're going to take a hard look in the mirror at ourselves and address any areas we might have inadvertently turned a blind eye to. Of course, we're not asking you to do something inauthentic; in fact, quite the opposite. Part of being relevant is fully embodying your authentic self. After all, when you know yourself better, you are better prepared to present yourself to the world in more profound and meaningful ways. In this section, we'll also address your personal brand, how you may (or may not) fit into various work cultures, and which one is the best fit for you.

We've invented a new term—*Mirrorset*—to define the necessary self-reflection skills needed to stay relevant. This is where your mindset, skillset, self-perception, and outward appearance all come together in a way that helps you appeal to the right audience at the right time. It's not about pretending to be something you're not; rather, it's about fully understanding who you are and presenting the best parts of yourself to attract and retain the perfect role for you. You can't afford to be oblivious to change. The world is changing every day—are you?

And now back to the question I love to ask: *Would you hire you?*

MANAGING YOUR FIRST IMPRESSION

You never get a second chance to make a first impression.

—Will Rogers

E very one of us has a story of a disastrous first impression—where we've gotten off on the wrong foot with someone, whether it's as benign as getting someone's name wrong or the familiar horror stories courtesy of social media. One story that sticks in my mind is about a man who was driving fast to get to a job interview on time. Someone was driving slowly in front of him, so he cut him off and flipped him the bird for good measure. Clearly, this driver suffered from the "I'm so import- ant" syndrome we described in Mindset: "My needs are more important than your time." Misson accomplished; he made it to the building five minutes faster. But when he arrived for his interview, he realized that the person he was interviewing with was the *same man he had just flipped off.* Unfortunately for him, the man recognized him, too.

The moral of the story: You only get one chance to make a first impression.

It turns out that first impressions can be lasting—even if they don't tell the whole story. For example, that employee speeding on the way to the interview and flipping off a future boss may have had a bad morning. But how he reacted says a lot about his character and his response to stress—all fair game in the hiring manager's decision.

Research backs this up. A study conducted by researchers at the University of York in Great Britain found that facial impressions can be made in as little as thirty-three milliseconds.[1] This small amount of time is sufficient enough to be "consequential" to give people enough information to determine who they might choose as, say, a romantic partner. Within that time, research subjects seemed to assess whether someone is trustworthy or attractive, and to decide their "status" (meaning social and economic standing). First impressions make lasting impressions—even if they are biased. In fact, people make subjective and long-lasting judgments based on first impressions all the time—and it takes a lot less time than you think.

Princeton University researchers found that it made no statistically significant difference whether 100 students had 100 milliseconds to rate another person's attractiveness, competence, likeability, aggressiveness, and trustworthiness compared to those in another group who were granted as much time as they wanted to make an assessment.[2] In other words, people seemed to stick to their first impressions.

That is not to say that if you get off on the wrong foot you can't recover. Nor am I advocating that you judge someone solely on how they appear the first time you meet them. However, it's important to note that this is precisely what most people are doing *when they meet you* in an interview. That's the whole point after all: to assess whether or not you'll be a good fit.

Maybe you've had the same job for a long time, and you're concerned people have already decided who and what you are—that you really can't change now. *You can always change.* We'll get into how to update your image or make improvements a bit later.

For now, let's focus on how you can make a good first impression. Typically we "communicate" who we are in three ways:

1. *Visually*—through our body language, facial expressions, and wardrobe, hair, and grooming, etc.

2. *Verbally*—through the words we choose

3. *Vocally*—how we speak (our tone, accent, or inflection)

In another study of first impressions, researchers found that 55 percent of impressions are informed by what we see, but 38 percent are by what we hear (tone), and only 7 percent of people remember the actual words we speak![3]

This is both the good news and the bad news. If you tend to stumble over your words, people seem to be forgiving; but if you sound sarcastic, rude, loud, short, or even slow, people will remember that and attribute a personality (funny, mean, obnoxious, etc.) to you. But 55 percent of first impressions are based on *what we see.* Are you aware of how people see you—from how you sit and stand (do you jitter, fiddle with your hair and clothes, lean to one side), whether you make eye contact or avoid it, and how you communicate through your posture (do you slouch, slump, or stand erect)? Do you nod or give other verbal or physical cues that you are paying attention or do you repeatedly interrupt? Are your arms crossed in front of you? Do you look like you're nodding off or spaced out? Do you have a firm handshake?

There are other behavioral signs, too. Are you punctual and prepared? If so, how can you demonstrate that without expressing it verbally? After all, we know actions speak louder than words (we just read the science). Then there are the not-so-obvious ways we make an impression. When you walk in a room, do you make assumptions about who is "in charge" based on their gender? I can't tell you how many times I have witnessed someone walk in and start directing female colleagues to get them coffee or to take notes, or worse, ignore them outright or talk down to them as if they were subordinates. Consider whether you treat others differently based on an internal bias.

You might not even know when your first impression happens. One day a few years ago, I recall arriving at our office early. I could see that the person we were scheduled to interview that day had arrived even earlier, a good sign. However, as I sat in my car and observed her, my first impression took a rough turn. She appeared frantic and chaotic, even though she was early, as though she was in a panicked rush and couldn't find the obvious and clearly designated entry door. She paced up and down in front of the building, walking for several minutes trying to figure out how to enter the building. The more I looked, the more frenzied she appeared. Eventually, she saw the entrance and made it into the office. When I sat down with her for the interview, sadly, her personality matched the rushed and confused behavior she'd exhibited before we even met. There was no way we could have hired her. She was out of contention before she even got into the building.

Most employers will evaluate you from the moment you arrive, whether you're aware of it or not. Often, I ask my assistant, who checks in visitors, to give me their impression. Were the candidates kind, friendly, and considerate to someone who wasn't going to offer them a job, or did they treat someone who was "only an assistant" differently?

I know several leaders who observe how a person leaves their office. Do they take their empty water bottle and place it in the trash? Do they push their chair back in, or do they expect someone else to clean up after them? I like to take candidates out for a meal to see how they treat servers and what their table manners are like. You can tell a lot about a person over a meal. In a sense, we're all being evaluated, and it's crucial in our personal lives as well as the workplace.

Today, most interviews and meetings are conducted over video, usually by Zoom. Thanks to these online meetings, it's not just about how you dress and carry yourself anymore. Instead, your face fills a whole computer screen, which can be unnerving. Most in-person meetings seat people from a distance of three or four feet.

Aside from how you look, you also have to consider how you present your background office to people. Have you ever been in an online video meeting with someone whose office background was a disaster? How can they carry on a conversation with you while piles of papers and stacks of clothes and boxes litter the backdrop? It's not only distracting, it also speaks volumes about their self-awareness, their ability to organize, and how they present themselves (or don't).

Think of your office as part of your brand. It's not just about having a clean and neutral space; there is a pressure to show others how we exhibit our personality and sense of style within a 10 x 12 inch screen. If it's not possible to curate your office background in a cool and interesting way, then there are other options. For example, I use the blurred background feature on meeting apps all the time.

> "What you wear is how you present yourself to the world, especially today, when human contacts are so quick. Fashion is instant language."

> —**Muccia Prada**

IS YOUR PERSONAL STYLE HOLDING YOU BACK?

We all know that one person (or several) who found their style in high school and college and decided to ride that fashion wave for the rest of their life. I've seen female professionals who still rock bangles and scarves circa 1985—hoping that they will come back in style. (They might, but you'll still have to modernize a former trend.) I have watched men arrive to interviews dressed in baggy, brown, double-breasted suits bought in the early 1990s. And even after they're hired, they'll still show up to work in them—even though everyone else is casually dressed in jeans and polo shirts. Styles change, and office styles change—even by location. What works in a finance office in Manhattan may be very different from an art gallery in Miami. It falls to you to regularly update your wardrobe. Why? What you wear and how you dress communicates to others that you're aware of what's going on in the world around you. It communicates who you are, what you value, and what you care about. Most importantly, it communicates pride and self-confidence in yourself.

What does your personal style say about you? Or should I ask, what do you think it does? And what do others think of you? You may think you're "timeless" or "classic" but your younger peers may see someone whose dress is outdated or old-fashioned. For example, take Mr. Brown Suit; how might his Gen Z and Millennial colleagues see him? Do you think he can have a meeting of the minds when there is a blatant physical reminder that they are years apart in age and attitude? Fashion, whether we like it or not, either builds a bridge or accentuates a gap. It shows we're willing to meet someone halfway, or that we're stuck on opposite sides of the river.

FIVE SIMPLE TIPS TO MAKE YOUR STYLE RELEVANT
1. Observe others without judgment.
You may take a lot of pride in staying above or outside the trends, but have you done this for so long that you have no idea what cool people are wearing? When was the last time you observed what the younger

people in your office wear or how they style their hair (without judging them)? Are there elements of more current styles that flatter you and that you can incorporate? When you're going to an interview, review the company website for cues about style and formality. It's also okay to ask the hiring manager what the workplace dress code is like—or what they suggest wearing for an interview.

If you move to a new region and start a job there, have you researched or observed the local fashion trends? Vanessa Friedman, a style expert for *The New York Times*, explains: In places with large concentrations of people, like cities and urban centers, "a fashion ethos will emerge. One with its own language and staples borne of the dominant industry of the place, its climate, its value system and the visual makeup of the city itself: its colors, building blocks and history."[4]

For example, when I moved to Florida from Oregon, the local styles were drastically different—the climate and culture demanded it. I had to pack away the fleece and update my look. I know a guy who moved to California after living in the Midwest. He was used to wearing jeans, golf shirts, and New Balances to work; suddenly he was surrounded by peers wearing Vans, linen pants, cotton or graphic T-shirts, and even hoodies to the office. At first it felt uncomfortable to step out of what he was used to, but soon he began to enjoy the more casual vibe of his peers.

Every region has its own "dress code." You don't have to run out and buy an entirely new wardrobe, but you can play with it in your own way—trying out one piece at a time.

Friedman advises that if you're not too concerned with fitting in, dress can be an effective means of letting others know that you are new to a place and therefore unaware of local customs and hotspots and, as such, manage others' expectations. In other words, don't shy away from being the "new person" and signaling that you're looking to meet people. But don't resist evolving as you get settled.[5]

2. Make small changes over time.

If you just moved somewhere or, conversely, you've been at a job for a while and want to be more relevant, don't get a makeover and an entirely new wardrobe in one weekend. Any transformation should be gradual and authentic. Don't suddenly arrive with a new look à la Chevy Chase when he goes to Milan and buys a ridiculous Italian leather suit in *National Lampoon's European Vacation*. Often when you try too hard to fit in, you end up looking (and feeling) totally out of place, as if you're wearing a costume instead of actually being yourself.

Friedman suggests that the best method is making little gradual changes rather than completely and suddenly changing how you "telegraph your identity—which is, after all, the point of fashion." Instead, use your current wardrobe and make small adjustments over time. For instance, as she suggests, if integrating into a more casual environment, keep your suit jacket but trade out the slacks for jeans; keep the skirt but trade out the heels for sneakers. Contrarily, in a more formal environment, tuck in your shirt or wear a fun accessory that fits you. Wardrobe adaptation should be a gradual process of attrition.[6]

3. Ask younger peers, coworkers, or colleagues for their honest feedback.

If you're unsure how you look, ask someone you trust or admire what they think of your wardrobe or hairstyle. Their feedback may be painful to hear, but if you adopt a coachable mindset, you'll be grateful. Maybe you've been going to the same hairstylist for years and they always cut your hair the same way. Have a frank conversation with your stylist or barber and ask for something different, something more relevant and modern but that is still you. If you have children, ask them how you look. Trust me, they will have no problem being honest about what you need to update!

4. Hire a styling service.

There are several online styling services that will ask you detailed questions about your personal style, location, workplace, and wardrobe needs. (Think Stitch Fix for women or Stately for men.) These stylists will put together trending seasonal outfits that you can try on, buy, or return based on your preferences. You don't have to do it all alone.

5. Don't be afraid to step out of your comfort zone.

One of the biggest reasons people don't change is because it's uncomfortable. We don't like change—we like our old shoes, pants, and clothes because they make us feel safe. Sometimes, we don't even see ourselves in the mirror anymore; we've become clothes, makeup, or hair "blind." But if you're serious about staying relevant, you must be willing to step outside of what you've always done and do things a bit differently. The decision to stay the same may feel good (and safer) in the moment, but it may cost you opportunities and business.

THE DECISION NOT TO HIRE IS MADE INSTANTLY.

You can change your clothes—but if you don't know how to carry the outfit, it could go all very wrong. After all, the clothes and style only tell part of the story.

When Candace coaches clients she reminds them that the decision to hire someone is always a long and thoughtful process, but the decision NOT to hire someone happens in just a few seconds. In fact, I would argue it's instantaneous.

Many people are unaware of how others see them and how they make judgments about their energy and their age. Are they fumbling with their hair, fidgeting with jewelry, or reaching for their phone? It's amazing how many people still forget to turn off their phones while in an interview or an important meeting. It can happen to anyone, but it's also revealing to see how a person responds when it happens. Do they take the call? Do they apologize and quickly remedy the situation by turning off their phone? Do they make a small joke at their own expense to show they have a sense of humor? All these details can reveal a lot about a person's organization, flexibility, and ability to think on their feet.

ARE YOU RELATABLE?

At the end of the day, relevance comes down to relatability; this is especially true for more senior roles, such as directors, VPs, and C-suite leaders. We don't work in a world where everyone—or even most of the team—looks, acts, and talks just like us. What goes on in the workplace is the same as what goes on outside it—you are going to interact with every race, gender identity, nationality, culture, and age every time you venture out of the house.

You especially don't get to pick and choose who you talk to or relate to at work. You are paid to represent a company and act on its behalf. This means, in some ways, you have to check yourself a bit at the door. You don't have unlimited permission to say what you think, act how you feel, or dress how you want. At home you can dress for your own comfort and amusement, but an attitude of "This is who I am! Just accept it!" won't fly at work. While there are some non-negotiables when it comes to our sense of self, you have to adjust your natural inclinations to participate in society. In today's workplace, you are going to be confronted with people of different faiths, who look different, who speak different languages. You don't get to decide who you will or won't interact with based on your preferences; your workplace decides for you.

The main takeaway from this section is this: Do everything you can to avoid making a poor first impression. To keep your job, or stay relevant, remain neutral—and that means avoid standing out in a negative way.

"Elegance is not standing out, but being remembered."

—Georgio Armani

One question Candace asks herself when interviewing someone is: "If I got trapped in an airport lounge for three hours with this person—would I be able to have an enjoyable conversation? Would we have chemistry or would I get annoyed after five minutes? Would this person lose their cool and yell at the gate agents, or act frazzled and overwhelmed?" She can tell a lot about whether she can relate to a person—and maybe grow to like them—based on the answer to this question. We often underestimate how much our personality, communication (verbal and nonverbal), and subtle behaviors impact others. Being aware of the impression we make on people is vitally important. And it starts by taking a hard look at ourselves and asking the same question: Would I want to hang out with someone like me in an airport for three hours?

Exercise: Ways to Update or Improve Your Business Image

Update your wardrobe.

If you hate shopping, or just don't know where to start, sites like Stitch Fix and Daily Look can help build your wardrobe. These professional services provide personal styling advice and clothing purchases to men and women based on age, profession, and personal style preferences. They will start by offering a quiz to get to know you before making any recommendations. Then they'll ship outfits and accessories to you based on your stylist's recommendations, and you can accept them or ship them back at no cost. Alternatively, make a habit of going through your closet each season and tossing outdated or ill-fitting clothes.

Don't even know what your style is? Hire a stylist to help you find the best look for your shape, location, job, and lifestyle. Understanding your personal style and brand is part art, part science. If you can't find or afford a stylist, sites like udemy.com (www.udemy.com) offer thousands of low-cost courses on subjects like personal branding. A search for "improve your personal style brand" brings up over 58,500 online courses, each lasting from two to eight hours, including master classes from LinkedIn.com that cost less than twenty dollars. There are similar courses on dressing for success, with thousands of offerings from personal stylists and fashion designers.

Believe it or not, the social media site (and app) TikTok is full of advice on how to dress well, both from style influencers of any age (including yours) to people willing to tell you what you're doing wrong. This gets brutally honest feedback that you can opt out of with a swipe—unlike asking your kids what they think you should do differently. You'll have to sort through a lot of noise to get worthwhile advice, but you can start by following accounts that address style and business image to get some tips worth trying. And you may see cringeworthy habits you didn't know you had through the lens of a younger generation.

Aim for a variety of accounts that address different generations at work. These are usually equal opportunity satirists (although Gen X seems to get off easiest.) Watching might be painful, but instructive.

Update your professional profile.

Start by updating your head shot. If you can't afford to hire a professional photographer, you can create a better headshot using AI (https://instaheadshots.com/). Here's how it works.

Create a great headshot using your own photos. The AI generator creates the background, lighting, and smoothing (even adding outfits to flatter your coloring). The whole process takes about an hour and costs less than fifty dollars. Since your headshot will appear as your avatar in apps like LinkedIn, and in video conferences on Teams or Zoom (if you don't use a camera), this can be an instant image boost. It's you—only better.

Send emails with confidence and professionalism.

Use apps like Grammarly that use AI to assist with writing. Just as you would want to avoid typos and spelling errors in your resume or CV, you want to ensure your professional correspondence is free of embarrassing mistakes that might disqualify you from the hiring pool. There are many other tools that help you hone your business communication skills, correcting grammar and usage and making sure your message is hitting the right notes for your intended audience. It can save you hours of fretting and editing time, correct your mistakes, and check citations, if you're using them.

TEN TIPS TO BECOME A BETTER CONVERSATIONALIST

1. **Don't talk when someone else is trying to concentrate.** When a person is trying to concentrate (whether on their laptop, or other things), it might be best to let that person do his or her job. They might appreciate having some mental bandwidth left open to work on the task at hand without having to juggle a conversation.

2. **Make eye contact.** When you're in a room with strangers, notice whether anyone makes eye contact with you. People who are open to a conversation will typically give some sort of signal—the main one being interest. If they are looking at you, asking follow-up

questions, or offering their own stories and shared experiences openly, you can safely bet they want to be there. However, if someone consistently looks away, they may need a moment alone or may not be in the mood for idle chatter.

3. **Enjoy the silence.** You may be a highly extroverted person who truly likes to interact with others, but don't feel the need to fill every empty space with words. Even when you're with your significant other, you don't need to have hours and hours of steady conversation to prove how much you love or feel close to each other.

4. **Find common and neutral ground.** There's nothing more embarrassing than making a comment about a situation with a stranger in which you've said something unintentionally insulting. Perhaps you see a person who's unusually tall, short, thin, or heavy, and feel like sharing your opinion of their appearance with your seatmate on the bus. For all you know that seatmate (who seems "average" to you) has a family member or close friend who isn't quite so average. Presuming that you share a world view with someone because of proximity is a socially perilous assumption.

5. **Pause in between sentences.** If you release a steady stream of verbiage, you'll have no way of knowing whether the other person is interested in keeping the conversation going. Allow your conversational partner a chance to not only get a word in edgewise, but to bow out graciously if he or she desires.

6. **Don't overshare.** You may feel it's safe to reveal personal details to someone you'll "never see again" (such as someone on vacation or in a new place) but remember the six degrees of separation principle: For all you know, the person you've just confessed to about cheating on an exam is best friends with the instructor's spouse.

7. **Be open to deeper conversations.** If things are going well, your conversational partner may be interested in moving from small talk to something bigger.

8. **Don't talk too much.** According to *The Wall Street Journal,* most of us talk too much.[7] According to journalist Rob LaZebnik, you can take this simple test to assess whether you talk too much. "After your next long conversation with someone, estimate what percentage of it you spent talking. Be honest. No, you're already underestimating. How do I know? Because it's more fun to talk than to listen. Talking is like drinking a great Cabernet. Listening is like doing squats. Add another 20 percent to your total." LaZebnik writes that the optimal conversation flow is (no surprise) 50/50. Here's how you get there: Ask questions. Once the person has answered, ask more questions. Finally, if you simply must, tell your story in one minute or less. LaZebnik cautions, "I can hear you complaining already: 'One minute? But I need to include all the details.' No, you don't. Just get to the good part."

9. **Avoid unintentional stereotypes.** Perhaps you know (or think you know) one thing about a certain place someone is from. Please don't bring up that fact from that place to the person who is from there. For example, don't ask anyone from Wisconsin if they are a "cheese head" or ask someone from Boston if they "pahhk their cahhh at Hahvahd Yahd." When you start a sentence with "Do you/they really . . ." chances are you're at risk of offending someone with what may be an old and dated stereotype.

10. **Practice.** The website TheMuse.com offers plenty of tips and resources for becoming a better conversationalist. The magazine *Psychology Today* is also filled with articles on communication and even offers tips on how to start conversations with strangers.

WEEK 10

HOW TO BE AUTHENTIC AND STAY RELEVANT

> Authenticity doesn't just mean you're not filtering what you're saying, it's about being able to know and access the best parts of yourself and bring them forward.
>
> —**Amy Cuddy**

BE YOURSELF—WITHIN REASON.

Over the past decade, there has been a trend toward "authenticity" in the workplace. We've already established that the days of wearing matching three-piece suits and adhering to strict dress codes are gone. Now people are invited to show and share their unique style, personality, and opinions in the workplace. The new generations, especially—Millennials, Gen Z, and Alphas—are used to and have been encouraged to share and be vocal about their thoughts, feelings, and opinions. Those of us who are Gen Xers and Boomers, however, come from a time where we spoke only when we were spoken to. We learned to park our personalities and issues at the door at school and then at the office when we started out. Each generation is comfortable with what they grew up with, but neither is completely right—or wrong. There is a middle path where Boomers, Gen X, Millennials, Gen Z, and Alphas can communicate with each other in a way that feels *authentic* while still remaining workplace friendly and relevant.

To do so, each group has to get past the labels—yes, even the generational labels of Boomers, Gen X, Millennials, Gen Z, and Alphas! While labels can help identify age groups and serve as a quasi-shorthand for our differences, they can also put us in a box that keeps us attached to a fixed mindset and identity. It's not just generational tags we cling to either. Our identities are attached to our political parties, religion, relationship status, gender, race, sex, nationality, illnesses—and that's just the big picture. When we divide ourselves by interests, sports teams, musical preferences, diets, and even departments within our organizations, the gap only widens.

It's okay to be proud of where you came from, what you care about, and what you do. I am not suggesting you hide or pretend to be something different than who you are. However, there is a particular risk in attaching yourself too much to one identity. When we strongly identify with one aspect of our personality, we tend to feel personally attacked if someone disagrees with us or sees things differently. Our fixed mindset, which we worked so hard to overcome in many areas of our life, gets stuck in a repeating loop when we feel criticized or reprimanded for something we or our affiliated group did. Perhaps you've heard some version of this: "If you criticize Gen X/Boomers/Panther fans/Floridians/ etc., you are criticizing *me!*" And the converse can be true as well. You can attack someone simply by their affiliation to some group, without ever knowing the person. That's why broad-sweeping observations can be so harmful. If you're tempted to start a sentence with "Everybody knows that . . ." you may be about to step on someone's toes.

What happens when people spend a lot of time anticipating perceived attacks? Naturally, they become defensive. There's an increasing pressure to come out and tell everyone about every aspect of their life and personality in advance as a form of self-protection. Recently, I sat down with a prospective employee and asked him, "So tell me about yourself." I thought he would start by talking about relevant job experiences or interests related to work. This was a job interview after all. Instead, he told me his political affiliation. I had no way to respond to that and was not sure what he hoped to get out of sharing it. Did he want me to say, "I am too!" Or did he want me to disagree with him and get into an argument then and there? It seemed he said this for two reasons: 1) to test me (and see if I was on "his side" or not) and 2) to self-protect. If I didn't hire him, he would have (in his mind at least) a ready-made excuse. He could tell himself and his friends that I didn't hire him because he was in his preferred party, and not because he wasn't qualified. There are so many ways to answer my question that could have expressed who he was as a person, what he valued, and how he might show up in the workplace. But that was neither the place nor the method.

If you want to be true to yourself, your beliefs, and identity, there is a way to do so that keeps you both authentic and relevant. It requires some heavy lifting—and you have to be willing to move beyond your wardrobe choices, your affiliations, and look at how you show up in the world in a broader context. When we think of "authentic" people—we tend to think of genuine people who are who they say they are. They do what they promise. We can predict how they will behave based on previous actions.

Candace says it's about being consistent. "The word 'integrity' evolved from the Latin word *integer*, meaning whole or complete. I don't change how I act based on my moods; I choose how I show up in the world, and people don't ever have to worry about which Candace will show up today." The modern meaning of *integrity* is synonymous with the words *incorruptibility*, *soundness*, and yes, *authentic*, which the dictionary defines as "not false or imitation: real actual" and "true to one's own personality, spirit or character."[1] When someone or something is real and/or true, we can expect that it will be that way again and again. In other words: We trust that when someone is authentic their behaviors will be consistent, dependable, sound, and incorruptible. For example, when people greet Candace they can expect she'll be wearing her signature black clothing, something that signals her East Coast business roots. She's always on time, prepared, and never misses a deadline. She comes to the point quickly. Her team and her clients know what to expect when it comes to her behavior and demeanor.

Now this can be great if behaviors and actions are work friendly, but they can backfire when they're not. This brings us back to: "Oh, this is just who I am! I am always dressed to be comfortable, instead of to impress. Deal with it!" Or "I am just a few minutes late! That's just who I am! It's not the end of the world." People who are late or always seem to flake out on the team may be living "authentically," but it's not the best version of themselves, let alone one they should draw attention to. Another example is if you describe yourself as a "straight shooter," someone who "tells people like it is." While that personality reads as "authentic" to you, it can be seen as abrasive, intrusive, and tactless by others. You may be offending people, whether you're aware of it (or intend to) or not. If you're this kind of personality and claim to never have seen the above signs, you might not be paying enough attention. (Something that may need work on your part.)

Workplace authenticity and communication experts for the *Harvard Business Review*, Lisa Rosh and Lynn Offermann, warn that self-disclosure, if not handled with tact and a deft touch, can backfire. When honest thoughts and feelings go against cultural norms or the beliefs of the person you are sharing with, it can damage your reputation, alienate colleagues, create distrust, and diminish teamwork.[2]

In their decades as organizational psychologists consulting on leadership development, team building, and communication skills, Rosh and Offermann have studied hundreds of cases where people who thought they were just "being themselves" rubbed others the wrong way or were unaware of how their stories or behavior impacted those around them.

Have you ever told a self-deprecating joke, only to be met with blank stares? Have you teased someone, thinking you were "only being funny," but could tell it went too far and hurt someone's feelings? Or have you been oblivious to people's reactions only to be called in by a manager or HR after the fact to find out you indeed took it too far and someone is drafting a formal complaint? Most of what flies at home or in casual conversation with friends doesn't pass muster in today's workplace. You have to pick and choose the parts of yourself you share with your team members. And to do this, you have to have a certain level of self-awareness; that is, according to Rosh and Offermann, "knowing who you are, your values, emotions, and competencies," and, most importantly, how others perceive them. "Only then can you know what to reveal and when," they add.[3]

You share your values, emotions, and competencies through communication, both formal and informal. How you speak to others and what you say to them matters. (Candace says, "I'm a writer. I believe words matter. In fact, every word matters.") Rosh and Offermann classify various people who seem to lack self-awareness as "oblivious, bumblers, or open books."[4] Those who are oblivious have no idea how they appear to others. We all know someone who claims to be one thing, but whose words and actions say something else altogether. Have you ever had a boss who claims to be "collaborative" and expresses they want their employees to voice their opinions and take the lead? But in reality they act as micromanagers, never listening to anyone's opinions but their own. Do you know a friend who claims to be a terrific listener, but every time you get together they don't stop talking long enough to take a breath, let alone listen to someone else? We all know bumblers, ramblers, and the person who takes too long to get to the point. They may love to tell a story but they have no idea that everyone around them is bored, can't follow it, or has their own story to share.

Then there are the "open books," or what I call the "oversharers." This is someone who trauma-dumps their entire life story within twenty minutes of meeting you. Or someone who feels the need to tell you every single detail of every annoyance that happened to them during the day. It can be tedious and exhausting to listen to.

Conversely, there are those people who, no matter what attempts you make to get to know them, remain unknowable or inscrutable. If you ask them a question, they offer one-word answers—it's yes, no, or just a simple "good." And then there are the people who are always "fine." No matter what you ask them, they're "fine." Their dog just died: "I'm fine!" They lost a big deal: "I'm fine!" Their life is falling apart at home: "I'm fine!"

There is more than one kind of wall people use to lock others out. Inscrutable is one version; another is a blast of blinding sunshine that is impenetrable—and exhausting for others. I work with someone who is always "terrific!" They constantly feel like they have to say they're doing great; they also serve as everyone else's cheerleader. I don't think I have ever had an honest conversation with this person. I wouldn't know a good day from a bad day for them, and that's not always a good thing. Why? Because as a leader, I want to trust that when I talk to someone, they can be themselves and will share what is really going on. I don't need everything to be candy-coated to be able to digest the news. It's very hard to trust someone if you feel you are never getting a straight answer—only the happy answer.

If you're an inscrutable person (of either kind), people may have difficulty getting to know you. This too may hurt you in the office setting. There is a fine line between oversharing and sharing just enough to make you appear real—knowing when to share and what to share is important. If you're giving a presentation, it's a great idea to start with a story—a personal story or anecdote will usually captivate an audience if it has a point related to the topic or theme. For example, if you give a keynote about entrepreneurship, instead of rattling off a bunch of stats and numbers, share how you got started in business and overcame your early setbacks. That would be very relatable for your audience.

Where you might cross the line is sharing how you were sued or had an unreliable employee—anything that pulls the focus off your important content or makes people question your authority or ability to lead. I strongly suggest leaving those stories out of your presentation. One way to know whether you're straying from the topic is to practice your talks or presentations beforehand; run them by a few trusted colleagues who will give you an honest critique.

FIVE TIPS FOR MORE RELEVANT AND AUTHENTIC COMMUNICATION

We have all made blunders and maybe even come across as insincere from trying too hard. All is not lost. You can make a comeback by owning your missteps and working to build a better sense of self-awareness. Here are five ways to improve your authenticity and relevance when you communicate:

1. Build a warehouse of self-knowledge.

The best way to be authentic is to truly understand both your strengths and weaknesses in relation to your ideas, opinions, beliefs, and stories. This includes taking a thorough inventory of your upbringing, work experiences, values, opinions, ideas, and views of the world. What do you feel comfortable sharing with family and friends, but not at work? Then ask yourself, why?

Is there a moment when you wondered if the ideas, stories, and opinions you share with peers may not be suitable for the workplace? Or, conversely, do you feel uncomfortable sharing at all? Would you say your peers know anything important about you? Have you sensed people's frustration when they can't seem to connect with you? Or have you found that you come on too strong for most people?

Candace was once in an interview with someone who delivered a very lengthy description of himself, which included his political affiliation and beliefs (and the fact that he enjoyed red meat and cigars). After the interview, Candace asked the gentleman why he put those modifiers out there so publicly, when they didn't directly relate to the job he was applying for. His answer was: "I only want to work with people who will accept me for who I am. If they don't like it, I don't want the job."

This was a very clear boundary this person was creating; I'm sure he'd describe it as being "his authentic self." While it seemed to suit him personally, I don't advise it. Not everyone will share your political beliefs, and it's usually not relevant to the work you need to accomplish together. While everyone has a right to their political and social opinions, this candidate was signaling his lack of tolerance of people who *might think differently from him.* If he only wants to work with people who think like him, he's narrowing his opportunities to become employed—and to grow as a person. Unless he's looking for work in a political role, this information would probably not be relevant. Rather, it may be drawing unnecessary attention, and not the positive kind.

That's why Candace recommends removing religious, political, and other affiliations that don't relate to the job opportunity from your resume. Even if you're proud of them, they can be a red flag to a recruiter who's looking for candidates who will fit into a culturally diverse team or who will be able to serve clients with specific expectations or backgrounds. Give yourself a chance to make a positive in-person impression before you decide to share too much of your out-of-office life.

2. Do not overshare personal details.

This is going to sound harsh, especially to readers who are used to sharing their personal life online and with each other, but—just don't do it. There is a time and a place to share your personal stories, and the office is not it. You may think sharing the details of a date gone bad, your divorce, your evil stepmother's interference, or how sick you got from the six espresso martinis you had Friday night might endear you to people, but they can also be a real turnoff. As Rosh and Offermann state, "Sharing too much personal information too quickly breaks all sociocultural norms of behavior, making one appear awkward, needy, or even unstable."[5]

Now, I am not saying you have to keep your mouth shut about your personal life, but no one needs all the details. "I had a great weekend." "The kids are with their mom for a couple of weeks." "I'm making some changes for my health." Those sentences don't need amplification, even if someone asks.

Neither should you be the one who presses others about personal details of their life. I had one colleague ask a new mother who had just returned to work, "Are you breast- or bottle-feeding?" The new mother looked mortified. She was preparing for a meeting and was blindsided by both the timing and the intrusion. Clearly, it was a topic she wasn't ready or willing to talk about, and for good reason—it was totally inappropriate. There are other ways to inquire about a new mother and her baby—and asking about a woman's body is not one of them.

Remember it takes time for people to get to know you, trust you, and feel ready to open up to you. Asking someone about any body part, health condition, family member (if you don't know the relative personally), relationship status, gender, sexual orientation, or past relationships isn't advisable. Most personal information comes up organically over time and is only revealed when someone feels comfortable enough to do so. They decide if, when, or ever. You don't have to wait years before telling colleagues anything about yourself—if you notice others sharing their stories over lunch or at a meeting and it's natural to do so, then share. Be sure to spend time listening, too—it's through listening and observing that we learn about the team culture, how others feel about sharing, and what is customary and safe to share.

3. Consider the relevance of your story to the task.

Candace taught a communications course for undergraduates at a local university for seven years. She told her students that when you decide to share stories with an audience, your goal should always be to make a connection. That means knowing your audience and using empathy to find what will help them understand you and themselves better, or to understand the situation better. Stories should be short, meaningful, and should leave your audience feeling more connected to you—or to each other. The same is true for public speaking, business presentations, and less formal conversations.

It's important to stop and ask yourself the following questions before sharing:

- What is my mission here? (To entertain, inform, enlighten, encourage, instruct, or make a connection?)

- Another way of saying this is: *Why* am I sharing this? (Is it just about me? Or is it also relevant or interesting to the people I'm talking to?)

- Is it to get people to like me (or at least understand me)?

- Is it to prove something to someone? (Use with caution, if at all.) Am I trying to one-up someone? (Yikes; please don't start this habit.)

- Do I have imposter syndrome? Am I trying hard not to let anyone see I am vulnerable or discover that I don't know what I am doing? (If you can feel yourself trying *very* hard, you're probably trying *too* hard.)

- Do I genuinely have experience and information that someone else would benefit from knowing? (This is insight that may take time to develop; you'll have to learn to read the room and absorb feedback.)

- Am I making sense, telling my story in a way that's easy to follow? Am I advancing how others understand the concept or situation? Or do they seem confused? (This is where you should stop and start over, if possible.)

- Am I trying to be seen as friendly (not difficult) and likeable? (Hopefully, this is always part of the goal of the story. But it's impossible to control that outcome.)

Typically, I have found that when you are trying to be liked, you try too hard and come off as insincere. Candace recalls an important business meeting with a team of executives from Atlanta. At lunch, she asked the man seated next to her if he was a Braves fan. He replied that yes, he was. If you know Candace, you know she's a diehard Braves fan, and she replied enthusiastically that she loves the team. The executive asked her who her favorite player was—and how she thought he was performing this season.

This was a friendly conversation starter. But it was, she reflected later, also a way to weed out insincerity. If she'd been able to name a team member, but been unable to discuss his batting or fielding performance, she'd have been dismissed. Candace never forgot that lesson; be sure you can back up whatever you bring up.

I've seen this very thing happen in my company's hallways recently. We see a lot of young people wearing vintage rock band T-shirts. If a younger person is wearing a T-shirt with a band logo on it, an older person might challenge them with, "Oh you like AC/DC? Name three of their songs."

If you feel inferior, thinking you have something to prove to someone, you may come off as defensive, or worse, an unlikeable, condescending jerk. (See "Yikes" above.)

Remember my coworker who had the piles of work and ran around telling everyone how much she worked and how busy she was? Not one of us was convinced by her behavior; it didn't feel authentic at all. We knew she had adopted the persona of a martyr to prove to everyone how much she was needed. The amount and type of work she was doing wasn't adding value to the company; it was a performance that exhausted her and made her less likeable as a team member. Rather than learn new and updated, time-saving practices, she spent her energy lamenting her workload and how underappreciated she felt. She won no friends this way. But she lacked the self-awareness to make the necessary changes.

There were lots of other ways for her to build rapport with peers and show she was a valuable member of the team. I've found the best and surest way to make yourself relevant is to be competent at your work. In other words: Do Your Job. You don't need to do a lot of explaining or make excuses if you're doing the work. Your work speaks for itself.

There are plenty of ways to build bonds and strengthen connections. You can talk about books, local sports, events, and restaurants in your area. One foolproof way to connect is to ask people about themselves (rather than tell them about yourself). Ask what their hobbies are outside of office hours, what they like to eat and where the best restaurants are. Ask what they're listening to (books, podcasts, or music) and what they like about it. I work out with colleagues who have a shared love of physical fitness and training. Fitness is a great equalizer, and people who share a passion for a particular workout or sport will find lots to talk about. You can be yourself—be authentic—and share the things you love without becoming a bore or putting people off. (See the end of the chapter for the "Am I Oversharing? Tip Sheet" if you are not sure when it is appropriate and relevant to share your stories.)

4. Be honest and sincere.

To be considered authentic, you need to be honest. And while this should be a given, you'd be amazed how many people lie at work. Trust me, when you lie, people know, they always know. In her article in the *Harvard Business Review*, "Why People Lie at Work," Liz Kislik writes that there are three main reasons why people lie at work: The first reason? "Fear of upsetting someone or triggering conflict."[6] This is an old survival mechanism from childhood to keep the peace at home. Somewhere, these people learned to stretch the truth to avoid punishment. In the workplace, this results in fudging the numbers, telling someone you never saw that email or received the document, exaggerating hours billed or worked, claiming you did something (then rushing off to actually do it before anyone finds out), and many more dubious acts.

Even small lies can break relationships. Consider the proverb "Fool me once, shame on you. Fool me twice, shame on me." Once trust is broken, it's almost impossible to repair. It doesn't take much, but if you're constantly telling "Big Fish" stories, inflating your resume or skills, or being dishonest about your shortcomings, you will be found out. If you make a mistake, come clean early. Apologize. Ask for help. Make it right. And learn the lesson.

The second reason people lie is because they are afraid to reveal their inadequacies or mistakes. They don't want to appear ineffective (or irrelevant), so they lie, cover up, blame others, and offer excuses. Candace worked with someone who could never admit he'd made a mistake. Never. It was always the equipment, the contractor, the weather—he had a million excuses. Her favorite was the day he walked in thirty minutes late to a (long standing) staff meeting. He'd missed his spot on the agenda (an important update), but instead of being apologetic, he was belligerent. He walked in with a to-go cup of coffee and announced to the room: "Sorry I'm late, but apparently [major restaurant chain] can't manage to serve a line of customers in less than forty minutes." Rolled eyeballs and stony silence rang throughout the room, which, as always, he paid no attention to. Not his fault; not his problem.

Just be honest. If you want to stay relevant and authentic, come clean and then make amends. Offer ways to help right the wrong. (The wrong being what others perceive, even if you still think you're right.)

The third reason people lie is simply because they want to get ahead at all costs. These are the status climbers, the take-no-prisoners-never-admit-defeat types. Somehow, even if they lose, they call themselves the winner. Kislik calls it creating a "fog of mistruth"—some people are so adept at lying, even though everyone knows they're lying, they really believe others are letting them get away with it. And in some ways they can because the liar confuses people so that they don't know what is up and what is down anymore. Many habitual liars believe they're entitled to untruths because "everybody does it." Everybody fakes their numbers, cheats on their golf scoresheet or their tax returns, or lies on loan or job applications. This tactic may work for a while, but it will eventually catch up with the liar.

5. Understand your environment and context.

Not every corporate culture is the same, and not every country or region shares the same ideas about what is deemed acceptable. Again, it's important to do your homework and research the company for which you are interviewing. Use online sites like LinkedIn or Glassdoor to learn about a company's culture. Research articles your boss or manager has written—what do they deem appropriate to share? If you're traveling to a certain region of the U.S. or outside of the country, make a point to read articles on cultural norms. For great topline advice on cultural norms like being on time, accepting and giving gifts, greetings, and business negotiations, Candace recommends *Kiss, Bow, Shake Hands: The Bestselling Guide to Doing Business in More Than 60 Countries*, by Terri Morrison and Wayne A. Conaway.

Even in the U.S., every region has a style, and within that region are businesses with diverse cultures and customs. Don't expect everyone to adapt to your way of doing things. Learn your company's culture—and the region's as well—and adapt accordingly. (We will cover this in depth in the next chapter.)

Exercise: Which version of you are you?

In the movie *The Naked Jungle*, Charlton Heston says, "Each man is three men: What he thinks he is, what others think he is, and what he really is."[7] I agree it's true that there are always three versions of yourself in play, even if you're not aware of them.

The person other people think you are.

The person you think you are.

The person you really are.

For this exercise, I want you to compile a complete picture of yourself. Ask your friends to describe you using ten words—funny, athletic, charming, happy, humble, arrogant, etc. While you solicit this feedback, write down in your own words how you wish people saw you.

Now I want you to be very honest with yourself. Write down how you really are. What are you proud of? What are you not so proud of? What do you hide from others? What do you wish you could show more often? What areas of your life do you wish you could improve? How have you grown or changed over the past few years?

How others perceive you may give you some insight here. You may be startled by some of their responses—did they take you by surprise? If they were negative, or weak praise, do they have you all wrong? What can you do to amend this portrait of yourself others have drawn for you? What are you holding back? Or what are you doing that is putting people off?

You might find that people see things in you that you would not have claimed. Confident, when you often feel scared and uncertain. Strong, when inside you're hanging on by a thread. Nurturing, when all you're doing is making sure everybody's okay, as anyone would.

Is there a disconnect between how others see you and how you see yourself? If so, you may want to engage with a communication coach so you can help close that gap.

THE "AM I OVERSHARING?" TIP SHEET

This tip sheet provides helpful guidelines to keep you on track, or at the very least keep you from those *Yikes!* moments. Candace came up with a quick checklist you can use when you feel the need to share your feelings, tell a personal story, or get something off your chest. You can also use it when you're heading out to an interview, a lunch, gathering, or meeting.

- **Who** are you sharing with? Can you trust their discretion? If this became general knowledge, would your reputation or brand be damaged?

- **Why** are you sharing this? To get attention? Sympathy? To vent? To connect with someone or show solidarity? To get advice or help? If you're not sure why you're sharing, think carefully before you speak.

- **When** are you sharing this? In the heat of the moment? Before things get out of hand? After reflection and a cooling down period? Is it a funny story about something that happened a while ago? (Tragedy + Time = Comedy, after all.)

- **How** are you sharing this? There's a world of difference between telling a work buddy "I'm ready to tell my new supervisor where he can shove it" and telling your boss "I have some concerns about the new procedures and I'm hoping we can talk them through." Make sure that you are controlling your message and the way it gets passed around if that becomes an issue.

- Ask yourself these questions:
  - Is this my buddy—or my boss?
    - ☐ Buddy: Maybe share.
    - ☐ Boss: It depends.

- º Is this a work friend—or a team member?
  - ☐ Work buddy: Probably share.
  - ☐ Team member: It depends.
- º Is this issue work related?
  - ☐ Yes: Maybe share with a work buddy or team member, and/or boss.
  - ☐ No: Maybe share with a work buddy or team member, but probably not with your boss, unless your boss has expressed interest.
- º Is this issue affecting my performance on the job?
  - ☐ Yes: Share with a team member and/or boss if you need assistance or guidance. Share with a work buddy with caution—it may become gossip.
  - ☐ No: Share with a work buddy.
- º Can someone at work help with this issue? (Performance, workload, career path, etc.)
  - ☐ Yes: Share with a team member and/or boss, at the appropriate time. Sharing with a work buddy makes it fair game for gossip.
  - ☐ No: Don't share.
- º Does this story/issue concern very personal matters (something you would be embarrassed about if it was discussed without you around or that you don't want many people to know)?
  - ☐ Yes: Don't share.
  - ☐ No: Share with a work buddy and/or a team member.
- º Have I talked about this issue before? Does it tend to dominate my conversations?

      ☐ Yes: Stop talking about it until/unless it gets resolved.

      ☐ No: Share with a work buddy with caution.

- What do I hope to gain from this conversation?

      ☐ If you don't know; don't share.

      ☐ If looking for advice or sympathy; share with a work buddy with caution.

- Is this issue what I want to be known for? Is this how I want people to think about me or talk about me?

      ☐ No: Don't share.

      ☐ I'm not sure: Don't share.

      ☐ I don't care: Share with caution but update your resume.

CULTURE COUNTS

A culture is strong when people work with each
other, for each other. A culture is weak when people
work against each other, for themselves.

—Simon Sinek

Several years ago, our parent company, headquartered in Tokyo, sent us a senior level leader I'll call K-San. They wanted him to brush up on his English while acclimating to the U.S. customs and culture. K-San took to coaching right away and approached learning how to fit in at a job he intended to fully succeed at. One of the first things he did was shop for clothes in the U.S. that catered to people his age. In Japan, young professionals wear suits. I took him to Buckle, a clothing store, to buy jeans. And for someone who had never worn jeans before coming to the U.S., he adapted just fine to the casual style. Over time, he developed his own sense of style and accumulated quite the wardrobe of modern casual wear. He also went to the movies and spent time watching older movies, so he had some common cultural references with his peers.

But he didn't stop there. K-San was committed to becoming part of the U.S. team. After hours, K-San took the time to learn the rules of American football, recognizing that being able to discuss things they were passionate about (in this case, sports) would help him relate well with the people he would be working with and leading. He attended both professional and college games and watched videos on football strategy. He learned about specific players on teams and got to the point where he could talk about which quarterbacks were going to lead their teams to wins. He fully embraced being a fan. And it didn't stop with sports—he was literally game for anything we suggested. He even attended a Monster Truck show, where he drank beer and ate pretzels with some of our recruiters—and had a blast! K-San was all in—not just as an observer but as a participant.

Eventually, he went on to be a very successful leader at one of our sister companies here in the U.S. and is well liked by both workers and managers. There was no doubt in my mind that he would be successful. From the outset, we loved him. And not just because he was competent at his job, but also because he was so eager and amenable to assimilating into our (U.S.) CSI culture. Sure, we were all part of the same company, but as I've said before, each office, location, region, and even department will have their own culture—and it all takes some level of adaptation, whether you come from another country or not.

WHAT DO I MEAN BY CULTURE?

When I speak of "culture" in business, I am talking about the values, beliefs, and behaviors that define how a company, department, or region operates. They can be written (many companies have Values and Mission

Statements), but for the most part, culture is a set of unwritten rules that guide an organization or community.

In a way, the culture is like a company's "personality." It sets the tone for how employees dress, speak to each other, engage with clients and vendors, participate in work, and even what they talk about. Certain work cultures are more "professional" (full suits) while some are "casual"; others have a corporate vibe or a start-up culture; some can be competitive while others are more laid back. But culture is more than tone—it also affects how leaders make decisions in regard to everything from hiring, firing, leading day-to-day operations, to engaging with employees and the public. It also often makes or breaks a company—and employees.

According to the Glassdoor recruiting website, 88 percent of employees consider culture as being important to their overall satisfaction.[1] And according to a Deloitte survey, 94 percent of executives believe culture is a main driver of a business's success.[2] That is, they take their culture very seriously and find it critical to their overall success. So if you want to be relevant—it would be smart to do as K-San did and learn as much as you can about a culture so you can connect with your colleagues and your leaders. No company is going to change its culture or style to meet you where you are. If you want to be employed or stay employed, you'll have to adapt to the company's culture. And there are several ways to do it.

RECOGNIZING THERE ARE NO ROLLOVER MINUTES

Back in the early days of cell phones, phone companies wouldn't allow "rollover minutes"—that is, the unused time from the previous month—to be used in the next month. Similarly, as Candace says, "There are no rollovers" in culture. You don't get to take the culture from your last employer (or even department) to your new one. At every organization, and even within departments at that same organization, it is your responsibility to do your research and figure out what you need to do to fit in. In essence you have to "pretend" you are K-San—that you are coming from a foreign country and need to start over.

BECOME COMPETENT.

As a military wife, Candace has had a lot of practice at starting over. Every time she moved with her husband, she had to learn a new city: how to navigate local customs (and just plain navigate), adapt to the new nomenclature, brush up on local events and news, and make endless small talk to get to know people. Moving so often, she contends, offered her a unique advantage. Because she was forced to move and start over every couple of years, she didn't have a long-ingrained sense of "this is how it's done." Because her tenure at every job was so short, she couldn't afford to say, "at my previous company, they did it this way . . ." She knew intuitively that it wouldn't make her seem smart or fit in better. Instead, she needed to observe, learn, ask questions, and spend a lot of time mimicking what successful people did to get up to speed on how the new place operated.

It reminds me of someone we hired several years ago, Joyce, who had been out of the workforce for several years. She had a great background and had experienced success but made the decision to stay home with her kids. When she decided to rejoin the workforce, she realized she would need to start at a lower level than her previous title. Ten years out of the workforce was a long time. Although she had great experience, technology and recruiting methodologies had changed tremendously over a decade.

Instead of adopting a "this isn't how I am used to doing it" or "this is how I did it before" attitude, she took the approach of learning from the recruiters who were having current success. She spent time shadowing, asking questions, and learning how to use technology. She listened while others talked to clients and to candidates. I personally witnessed her take a ton of notes and incorporate what she learned into her vocabulary at work. Needless to say, she had plenty of quick wins. Combining her newly learned skills with her strong work ethic, Joyce climbed quickly up the ranks of the organization. She went on to become a well-liked and respected recruiting manager—and eventually, a division manager. One of the best ways to fit in is to be competent at your job—and you get there by being humble and willing to learn.

Both Candace and Joyce had no other choice—Candace had to move and make the best of her situation, and Joyce had to learn the new way of doing things or risk not being hired or promoted. You can't forget that part of "fitting in" and adapting is recognizing that each region, workplace, organization, and period requires a specific set of knowledge and skills. And you have to learn them if you want to stay relevant.

FIT IN BEFORE YOU STAND OUT.

I get it—everyone wants to be exceptional or different. Special. We want to make our mark in the world, or at the very least at our jobs. However, in our rush to stand out—or do things our own way—we can miss the signs that we're not adapting to the culture. For example, at CSI health and fitness are a big part of our culture. That's why we have a full gym onsite, with locker rooms, staffed with trainers who offer classes for a variety of fitness levels. We have employed some highly regarded trainers who are up to date with the latest HIIT classes and strength workouts. The classes are almost always full, and there is a strong sense of camaraderie among the staff who attend. In CSI's culture, we believe working out together is a great way to bond and feel a sense of accomplishment. Over the years, it has also become a way for people to form solid relationships.

One year, we hired a new sales guy who really resisted acclimating to our culture. Because he claimed to be a fitness guy (though he didn't look it), I assumed he would at least enjoy the benefits of our health-focused culture and would eventually warm up. Over time, everyone noticed that he came to the gym during the same times as the HIIT classes but would never participate—he wouldn't even talk to anyone. He would just do his own thing.

One day, the trainer called him out and invited him to join the class, but he said he'd been working out on his own for most of his adult life and didn't need a coach for motivation. He said what he was doing was working, and he was "good." However, he was actually in terrible physical shape. For all his working out, he didn't seem to have the results of someone who knew what he was doing. Not surprisingly, we came to see this same attitude in his work. He always knew better than the people he was working with. He resisted taking any direction and refused to admit he needed help when he clearly did. He also failed to recognize that we were building a culture of "teams"; working well (and playing well) with others was an important part of our organization as a whole. His decision to be a lone wolf and "stand out" didn't turn out so well.

DON'T BECOME A TROPE.

The comedian Jerry Seinfeld was notorious for the names he and his friends on the show *Seinfeld* would reduce others to, a shorthand based on how they looked or behaved. Man-Hands, Close-Talker, Low-Talker, or the infamous Soup Nazi. And it was never *a good thing*. In the workplace, there are all sorts of cultural and relational taboos and generally bad behaviors that will quickly get you labeled.

Often, CSI leaders will accompany our salespeople to meetings; no matter how long someone's been with the company, we think it's helpful to share feedback on their methods. One of the more seasoned salespeople—let's call him Old School—asked me to go on some calls with him in a nearby major city. When I arrived, he had printed out an itinerary, including directions to all the clients we were supposed to meet with.

"Why did you print all that and not use Waze?" I asked him.

"What's Waze?" he asked.

After trying not to look incredulous or ask, "Are you kidding me? Do you live under a rock?" I explained how it was an app like Apple or Google Maps—and there was no need to print directions.

He waved it off and said, "I'm Old School." Whether he understood it or not, that was part of his brand, and it probably put some unnecessary distance between him and his younger peers and clients.

During a conversation with a group of managers we had another "Old School" leader (let's call him "Archie Bunker") use a very outdated and inflammatory word for "biracial." He didn't realize he'd said it. When several people reacted, he stopped and asked what was wrong and it went downhill from there. Trying to dig himself out of the mess just made him sound even more outdated, and worse—racist.

We had another senior leader, "Hugger," who struggled with boundaries. He would often put his hand on a woman or randomly put his arm around her while talking. When someone pointed out that he was making people uncomfortable he said, "People know I don't mean anything by it." But did they? Could they even express it if they wanted to—especially with a senior leader? This type of behavior puts the company in a terrible position—not to mention the individuals who feel uncomfortable. He may have been allowed (or have gotten away with) that behavior in the past, but workplaces, thankfully, have changed. There are now clear boundaries about what is and is not acceptable.

It's not just inappropriate talking, hugging, or "old school" behavior that can make you stand out (and not in a good way). Over the years, we've had a number of people struggle trying to interact and relate to younger people in the office. We had one employee who started every lecture or soliloquy with, "Back in the day we would do _____" or she would say, "This was before your time . . . but we used to _____." People tended to avoid her because they didn't want to go down memory lane (again) or be lectured by someone on how they did it better.

To remain relevant, you want to do everything you can to avoid becoming someone who stands out for the wrong reasons.

And don't claim "ignorance" as an excuse. You may believe that "I didn't know that word was offensive" buys you a free pass, but it won't. It's your responsibility to know what is socially acceptable.

DRESS THE PART.

Appearances matter. We are going to dive deep into your personal brand in the next chapter (which is more than what you wear), but how you show up to the office, a meeting, or a client—whether on Zoom or in person—matters. Remember K-San from Japan? Imagine how people would perceive a full suit and tie in a casual work environment where most people wear jeans. It would have made him stand out, for sure, but it also would have made it very hard for him to make the connections he did. There are times when you have to adapt to other cultures within your own work culture. That is, you have to be on alert—and ready to pivot.

At CSI, we have clients all over the country and we spend a lot of time in front of those clients. We had an important sales presentation in front of a board of directors with a large health system in Boston. I encouraged everyone to "suit up" and dress more for what I call "the city" (as opposed to our Jacksonville, Florida, vibe). One of our "elder" leaders said he would be fine wearing his usual wardrobe. When I pushed back and reminded him how important first impressions would be, he doubled down on his usual old khakis with cowboy boots.

We found out later that the leaders prejudged us as we walked into the boardroom. Our elder leader's attire became a big part of their jokes about us later. We wanted to be taken seriously, but in their eyes, we looked like country folk who had come to the big city for the first time. It's not what I was hoping for going into that meeting.

When you always try to do things your way, you pull the focus to you—and who misses out? The team, and by default your organization. Do your best to go along with what others are doing. Yes, there are always exceptions to the rules; people will be quick to cite *Erin Brockovich*, showing up to a law office in a miniskirt, high heels, and a baby on her hip to ask for a job. In the end, despite her wardrobe, she helped take down a large California energy company. But what people forget is—she was the *perfect person* to reach out to all the working-class moms and dads in the California desert who were suffering from cancer and illness caused by the energy company. She wasn't "a suit" or a "big lawyer"; she was "one of them" and that's why she was able to get all the defendants to trust her. She understood her audience and what they cared about. And she cared about them.

Again, do your research. Be willing to be humble and take some advice—or in some cases, take one for the team. It wouldn't have killed my colleague to put on dress shoes and dress pants and to leave his cowboy boots and khakis at home. If he had, the client's conversation that night wouldn't have been about him or his choice of footwear, but rather, the work our team spent a great deal of time preparing to present.

SHOW UP FULLY FOR ANY ROLE YOU'RE IN—ON VIDEO AND IN PERSON.

Consider that how you look, behave, and act doesn't just represent you—it represents the entire company. We had a leader in one of our back-office functions who just couldn't adapt to Zoom video calls. As important as her role was, she would never appear on camera. We told her multiple times that people wanted—needed—to see her. Part of her role was developing rapport with her clients, both internal CSI staff and external clients. She didn't understand the importance of people seeing her; she didn't get that looking into her eyes, even through a screen, gave people a sense of confidence that she would handle situations and fix problems. When she did get on camera, she kept her head down and didn't make (virtual) eye contact.

She never understood that it wasn't just her that they needed to feel confident about—it was the role she held in our company as well. Eventually we had to move on from her; our reputation with clients was suffering since people started to say she couldn't handle the role.

Whether you are in a new workplace or your company is pivoting strategically (restructuring, changing leadership, or merging with another company), time marches on and technology, norms, and cultural references change. You need to be able to adapt.

FIVE TIPS FOR STAYING CULTURALLY RELEVANT
1. Stay informed.

Regularly consume a diverse range of news and social media (part of being relevant is knowing which social media platforms are relevant; they change all the time). This includes keeping up with your industry, global and local events, trends in entertainment, sports, and your local community. If you claim to know something—you better be able to back it up. We once had a recruit who talked big about his golf game. He claimed he knew it well and was great at it. Our CEO at the time took him at his word and tapped him to play in a tournament representing our company. Turns out he was awful; he had never played before and it was a disaster. He was fired after that, not because he was a bad golfer,

but because he was dishonest about something so basic and easily dis-
proved. No one trusted him after that.

Long story short: Don't pretend to be knowledgeable about something you don't know. Yes, it's important to fit in, but not if you have to
lie or embellish. Do your research, become as adept as you can at what
fits with your skills and experience, and then be honest about your capabilities and limitations.

2. Understand your audience.

It's vital to know your audience. Make sure you understand the company
you are applying to, or the new manager, new owner, or new division
you will be working for. Tailor your message to be both respectful and
relatable. Find out how they dress and what their cultural norms are.
(Everyone has access to Google.) If you are curious about how people
dress in certain areas or industries, consider using apps like Pinterest,
TikTok, and Instagram to search wardrobe styles in your destination.

3. Show respect by learning the right names.

The first signal of respect for another culture is learning the language.
You may not be a linguist, but you get exactly one shot at asking someone how to pronounce their name. After that, your mispronunciation
or mangling of their name will feel like a slight, at best—an insult at
worst. Candace once worked with someone with a complex last name,
made more complex when in writing. One of the senior managers in
the company thought mispronouncing her name was hilarious. It was
a not-so-subtle way of putting her down, and he thought he had a free
pass because "he just could never get it right."

The names you use matters. The same is true for technology, industry jargon, and even what you call other teams. When you say, "the screen thingy just disappeared again," you sound ignorant. Calling them "the girls on the third floor" instead of "the marketing team" makes you sound spiteful. Nomenclature is culture.

4. Keep an open mind and be willing to learn.

Be willing to challenge your own biases and assumptions. Be willing to listen to diverse perspectives—those younger and less experienced have something to teach you. If you're young, there is something to be learned from those older than you. A willingness to listen for understanding rather than the need to be right goes a long way.

5. Be aware of your work culture's ideas around inclusivity.

Make sure your language, content, dress, and actions all reflect your company's cultural norms, while respecting all people. We will get to this more in the next chapter about personal brand, but it's important to remember that just because you think, dress, believe, and behave in a certain way doesn't mean the rest of the world has to agree with you—or even like you. They have to respect you—and you have to respect others—but you don't have to agree on every issue to get along in the workplace. You can be thoughtful, aware, and curious about others without being offensive in your approach. Remember that although no one is under any obligation to follow anyone else's personal cultural norms or values, we must all treat each other with dignity and respect in the workplace.

MASTERING YOUR PERSONAL BRAND

Your brand is what people say about you
when you're not in the room.

—**Jeff Bezos,** founder of Amazon

Your personal brand is what people think you are. It used to be common to say that "your personal brand tells your story," but it is more active than that. Your brand tells the story that you have crafted, what you want others to know and think about you. It's how you control the narrative of what people say about you behind your back; by deliberately choosing the way you want to be perceived in the world and what you want people to think about you. Companies and products think about branding all the time.

For some, this might sound inauthentic or fake but I don't think of it that way at all. It's an important part of deciding mindfully how you're going to show up at the workplace and on social media. You have choices to make every day; once you decide what your brand is, whether it's the rebel, the troublemaker, the tough-guy CEO, or the empathetic leader, your personal brand will always precede you.

As a coach, Candace spends a lot of time helping her clients identify and form their personal and professional brand. She says that the essential questions employers are asking are: "What am I getting when I hire this person? Is she who she says she is? Can I count on her to do what she says, be who she presents herself as?" When crafting your brand, it can't remain aspirational—you have to be prepared to *become* and *live* who you present yourself as. Candace says, "Brand simply means that if you say you are, you are; what you say you do, you do. Essentially, it comes down to this: 'how you do anything is how you do everything.'"

What are people saying behind your back when you leave the room? Who are you? And are you *really* who you say you are?

If you think you're "above having a brand" or that you "don't have a brand" right now—you do, you're just not aware of it. And this week, we're going to help you realize that if you're not aware of your brand, or if your brand is not telling an accurate story, we can give you the steps to change that. Because, as much as I hate to say it—you are being judged and branded whether you like it or not. Your job is to get ahead of it and create a brand you wouldn't mind people recognizing you for.

A WORD OF CAUTION ABOUT BRANDING: THE DANGER OF PIGEONHOLING YOURSELF

In the show *Only Murders in the Building,* Selena Gomez's character visits a suspect's apartment. It is fully decorated for Christmas—as is he. He is wearing a sweater that depicts a present wrapped in a gaudy bow. The only problem is, it's months before Christmas. Everyone thinks he is obsessed with Christmas—it's definitely his personal brand. And he plays along for a while. That is, until he cracks and reveals he actually hates Christmas. It was an accident really—he made one post at Christmas and it went viral, and now he felt he had to chase that brand to be liked. He had literally and figuratively wrapped himself into a box he didn't want to be in and couldn't get out of. He felt he had to be this guy. The problem was: *He wasn't that guy. Not even close.* He became a caricature of himself, rather than his authentic self. And people expected his love of Christmas everywhere—not just on social media but in real life. He knew the unwritten rules of "personal brand"—you have to "be the brand." But, if it's not really who you are, the feeling of being a fraud will eventually catch up with you. If you present yourself one way, say in person and on social media, and you are not that way at work—people will be aware of it. Even if you think they won't—they know. People can sense inauthenticity, and they will recognize it when your actions don't align with who you present yourself to be.

IDENTIFY ELEMENTS OF YOUR PERSONAL BRAND.

There are many components that make up your personal brand. Of course there is your fashion style, but also the way you communicate: in person, in writing, and on social media. It's how you show up in the world—and what you choose to identify with your personality.

According to an article in the *Harvard Business Review*, both professional and personal success largely revolves around your ability to communicate and persuade others of your value, from job applications and promotion requests to dating profiles. "In today's world everyone is a brand, and you need to develop yours and get comfortable marketing it."[1] Jill Avery and Rachel Greenwald, the authors of the article, teach at Harvard Business School and created a several-step process that helps people outline their personal brand. I've modified it a bit and made it my own, but one step that I completely agree on is that when crafting your personal brand, you must define your purpose.

DEFINING YOUR PURPOSE

Some people refer to their purpose as their "why"—the reason why they do what they do. One way to think of your purpose is this: What kind of impact or difference do you want to make? What drives you? In other words:

Who do you want to serve?

How do you think you can make a difference in their lives?

What value do you think you will provide?

What qualities do you possess to do this?

This is the first step to understanding why you do what you do. None of us do anything without some sort of reason and reward (beyond getting paid, of course). You have to have a bigger reason for why you do what you do. Once you do that, you can truly understand who you are at a fundamental level. (We have created a complete exercise at the end of the book that breaks this process down.)

UNDERSTAND WHO YOU ARE: YOUR VALUES, EXPERIENCE, AND WORK/LIFE ACTIVITIES.

To build your brand and become more aware of how you're perceived, you have to start from the beginning—that is understanding your personal narrative and what people know about you. This is not just about your credentials, but also your behavior, actions, thoughts, and feelings—whether they jive with what others think of you. Another way to examine this is to ask yourself:

Who or what do you identify with?

Think of a common way you define yourself: "I'm a . . . Sports Fan/ Music Fan/Member of a Political Party/Region/Culture/Religion/ Gender/Etc."

There are a million facts about me that I could choose to embrace.

So it's the picking and choosing of the things that are true that I want to put forward as who I really am. But again, you have to be careful—you can take it too far, like our Christmas Guy character. Ask yourself: Do you *only* want to be known as a supporter of a particular candidate? Do you want that to be your entire personality? Do you *only* want to be associated with one team or band or be known mostly as a dachshund mom? We all contain multitudes, and it's important to think of yourself holistically.

So many of us unintendingly pigeonhole ourselves by what we choose to talk about, share on social media, wear, and openly advertise right down to the stickers we put on our cars, laptops, or even water bottles. We make our interests into our entire "identity." We may even be unaware of it. I had a friend from Oregon who moved to another state and began posting on social media how vastly different her new state was to the old one, particularly in regard to politics and social issues.

She came off as extreme and alienating—some would say polarizing. She was perceived as so obnoxious about it that it annoyed the people who may have agreed with her. Sometimes, too much is just too much. She had no idea about how people perceived her; maybe she didn't care because she felt justified in her own mind. And she's not alone.

It can be difficult to figure out how we look to others; that's why we recommend asking people you trust how they see you. No matter what you think you're doing, how it's being perceived and received can be very different. For example, I've always felt I was full of helpful advice. But I also realize that unsolicited advice can be experienced as criticism. What I perceive as "helpful" can be perceived as "critical" or "judgmental" by someone else.

It's important to cast a wide net and look outside yourself. What are others doing? What do you admire in them? What does the audience you're attempting to connect with appreciate and value?

BEING ABLE TO ARTICULATE YOUR STORY

I know I said brand isn't just your personal story. But your story is an essential part of your brand, and at some point you will be asked to create your own brand statement or story. Whether you're crafting a website for your business, setting up a LinkedIn profile, writing a cover letter for your resume, or answering questions at a job interview—you will have to tell a story. Every politician has a well-worn stump speech—it's the story they tell every crowd. It's the same script (with a few tweaks here and there modified for an audience), but by and large it tells the story the candidate wants people to hear and, in an ideal world, actually live up to once elected. Your personal brand story is your stump speech—it's essentially saying: This is who I am. This is what you will get.

So yes, a brand is more than your purpose, values, and experience; it's *also* your story. Everyone should have a "Tell me about yourself" elevator speech ready. If you're in a job interview or an office, chances are they have your resume or know your current role. An interview isn't the time to list all of the things you've done and places you've gone. Rather, it's time to tell your story.

A great rule of thumb when crafting your own story is to think of the writing advice: "show, don't tell." If you're a team player who loves getting along with people, mention the teams you're on and what you contribute to them or the successes you have had in them. Tell a story about the time that really proved or expressed your ability to play well with others. Or, if you're a self-starter who doesn't need a lot of external motivation, share that you run marathons and get up every morning at five to train—that you love a tough workout and challenge.

Think about political stump speeches—how they try to persuade people to follow, promote, and elect a person. Your personal brand statement should also be persuasive; it should resonate with your audience and introduce them to, or remind them of, who you are.

YOU MUST BECOME THE STORY.

In Avery and Greenwald's explanation of personal branding for the *Harvard Business Review*, they remind us that in every social interaction you have, be it small talk with strangers, conversations with friends, or job interviews, "people are forming opinions about you, . . . and consciously or subconsciously, you're advertising yourself."[2]

It's imperative that you are always self-aware and mindful of the messages you're putting out in the world. Are you an energy-sucking vampire? Every time someone asks how you are, do you complain or rant about something going on in your life, the news, or in the office? Are you the inexhaustible cheerleader who never has a bad day, even when their dog dies? Are you aware of your audience and do you take that into consideration when you speak? Do you constantly brag or use a virtual megaphone for all your achievements? Or are you a drama queen? Are you the coworker who always has a story about why they are late, the traffic accident that held them up, the technology that didn't work as advertised, or the coworker who didn't meet *their* deadlines? Candace once had a contractor she called Mr. 1000 Excuses. It was never his fault that he was running late. He always had some kind of excuse, from the elaborate to the mundane, and unfortunately, that became his brand. Remember: Everything you say and do communicates your brand story.

COMMUNICATING AND SOCIALIZING YOUR BRAND

We have been predicting the end of paper resumes for decades. We've talked about the fact that resumes look backward; while employers want to see your experience, they also want to know what you will be able to do for them now and in the future. So much of what you did ten, twenty, and even thirty years ago simply isn't relevant. And no young person wants to hear about how you "did things back then."

Our brand stories, also, should look forward. By now, everyone should have an online profile or, at the very least a LinkedIn profile, but there are other options as well. It should be obvious that you invest in and care about your online presence. Hopefully, you didn't set it up ten years ago, never touched it again, and have only thirty-seven followers or connections. Because it will be obvious to others that you're not using technology the way you could.

As soon as you apply for a job or reach out to a recruiter, the first thing they will do is look for you—and at you—online. They're going to visit your social media and LinkedIn profiles to learn what they can. That's what we do at CSI to figure out who you are and what you are. Keeping your online profile up-to-date is essential to staying relevant.

Applying online for a job, even if you have a killer online presence, is rarely going to land you a great job. That may sound harsh, but you're relying on an application or resume to do the work your network should be doing. Ideally, you should be applying through warm leads—people who know you and can recommend you. Reach out to your network—in person or on social media—and let people know you're looking for work. That is what gets you noticed.

I am more likely to trust a candidate coming highly recommended or referred from a peer. Granted, that is not always possible. But, as you move up in your career, you should have developed a large network that can serve as your safety net and your lead referral system. You need to look for as many opportunities as you can to network at casual events and formal career and professional events, where you can communicate your story.

RECRUIT OTHERS TO COMMUNICATE YOUR BRAND STORY.

Once you feel confident that you have captured your story—and you're ready to put it out there—you'll want to spread the message far and wide. You'll also need others to do that for you when you're not there in person. As Avery and Greenwald say, personal branding requires the input of others to add credibility to your stories and allow you to reach new audiences. You can't do it alone, so it's important to build a network of people and communities that can help you along.[3] They also suggest tapping thought leaders and influencers with actively engaged followers or users. Ask them to spread your brand story or message/expertise, whether it's on their pages, podcasts, blogs, or at their events. They suggest using "promoters" or those "actively invested in your success" who can help communicate your personal brand. This includes colleagues, bosses, and friends who will connect you with their own contacts and provide opportunities for interviews. Figuring out who you know, and who could advocate for you in rooms when you're not there, is incredibly important. And I can't express this enough—if you want others to do this for you—you have to do it for other people, too. Return the favor and recommend or promote others when they aren't in the room.

There are other ways to network, such as joining online and in-person groups, clubs, associations, organizations, and message boards. Putting your name out there often, in places where the people you are trying to reach are likely to find you, is an important part of the story-telling process. At the very least, you can brush up on your brand storytelling outside the professional/work world; at the very best, you may find your next opportunity.

YOUR BRAND DOESN'T HAVE TO BE STATIC.

The world is changing; if you want to stay relevant and be relevant, you have to constantly evolve and reinvent yourself. This includes how you dress and how you show up professionally and in the world. You must be willing to go back to the starting line and reevaluate who you are and what you stand for. It's perfectly natural to outgrow styles, friendships, people, passions, workplaces, positions, and interests—remember the previous discussion of priorities? Each serves a purpose for a time and a season, and sometimes we have to move on, to start over. Sometimes something external forces us to. Whether it's our own choice or someone else's, be prepared to start over again and again. The good news is you're not starting from scratch; you now have tools, lots of them, to help you stay relevant, no matter where you are in your professional journey or how many times you start over.

PERSONAL BRANDING EXERCISES

Creating your personal brand may feel like a daunting task, but it's an essential exercise if you want to take control of your career. In Avery and Greenwald's article, they suggest starting with your purpose in life. They call this your "through line," finding your significance to others and the answer as to how and why you have lived the life you have. Look for traits that define you whenever you face opportunity or adversity. Are there common denominators in your choices and experiences? Here are some examples:

- Grit, persistence, determination

- Risk taking (or a cautious approach)

- Joy, laughter, or fun as priorities

- Loyalty to family, friends, your teammates, your employer

- Creativity, imagination, innovative thinking

- Hard work, reliability, consistency in your character and your actions

You get the idea. As a personal exercise, think of a story or two that illustrates the characteristics you think of as your foundational values/strengths.

Avery and Greenwald write that the first step is to identify moments "when you've fully embodied the brand you want to have—those moments when you were positive, productive, authentic, made a difference, and stood out from the crowd."[4] Next, consider your resume—the experience, credentials, and achievements that make up your career path and define your success. Put them together in a sentence or two that would help a hiring manager understand what they're getting from you. Here are some examples:

- A financial services professional with twenty years of experience making people feel confident about setting and achieving their financial goals.

- A strong manager whose teams thrive because they've learned to work together on strategic goals and exceed performance measures.

- An imaginative creative professional with an MBA and a ruthless commitment to meeting deadlines and bringing the company's brand vision to life.

Finally, ask others to describe your brand. Partners, spouses, close friends, teammates—even your kids—can come up with a few words that describe you at your best. (And maybe at your worst.)

Ask "what do you admire about me?" Most people you ask will be able to come up with a word or phrase or two that describes how they see you. Take some time to see how their description fits in with your view of your own brand. Ask yourself:

Does it enhance or expand it?

Contradict it?

Surprise you?

Make you think?

Then experiment with incorporating it into your own branding statement.

DISCOVER YOUR "PRACTICAL GENIUS."

In his foreword to Gina Rudan's book, *Practical Genius: A 5-Step Plan to Turn Your Talent and Passion into Success,* author Kevin Carroll writes, "What makes [people] practical geniuses, as Gina would describe them, is the unique combination of heart and smarts they possess, as committed to the joy, humor, and creativity in their professional lives as they are to excellence in the work they produce. You know one of these geniuses when you see one, believe me."[5]

Gina Rudan writes that becoming a practical genius is about "intertwining your strengths, your passions, and your values to establish the complete, original formula for your success."[6]

Here's a helpful exercise: Think of three words that describe you. Then try to explain why these three words come to mind. Another approach is to craft a "brand statement" or story. If you have more than three words, that's fine—the point is to be able to articulate what matters and what you value (or want others to value).

Next, Candace and I share our own strengths, passions, and values. I have chosen three words and Candace has shared an example of a brand statement.

My Strengths:

- I do the right thing, even when it's difficult.

- I am deliberate and slow to make judgments; I take my time in making assessments.

- I have integrity. One of my favorite quotes is: "People of integrity expect to be believed and when they are not, they let time prove them right."

Passions:

- I am committed to my well-being, both physical and mental.
- I enjoy sharing the good things I've been lucky enough to experience.
- I think it is important to give back to our community to help it thrive.

Values:

- I put my ego aside so I can see clearly and make thoughtful decisions.
- I treat people fairly and give them every opportunity to succeed.

I also chose three words that define my brand—how I show up for my work and my people. While not all-inclusive, they are foundational to who I am.

Adaptable

As my career has grown, I've proven to myself that I am adaptable. I've been fortunate to have experienced many different types of roles, both as an individual contributor and as a leader. I have worked for difficult people, and I have worked for generous people. I've worked for small, private companies as well as big, public companies. In each situation, I had to find ways to stay true to myself and hold my core values while still operating at a high level to achieve the goals of my boss and the company.

Generous

I've never forgotten where I come from and how fortunate I am to be where I am. I realize that people throughout my career have given me opportunities and allowed me time to figure things out. I try and do the same with others. Whenever I think I can be helpful, I try to be generous with my time and advice.

I also believe strongly in giving back, and therefore have always found a tremendous amount of joy in helping people experience some of the cool things I've been able to experience in my life. Generosity, for me, can be in the form of material things or in the sharing of my time or the wisdom I may have accrued in my career.

Dependable

I learned early in my life (thanks to great parents!) that if you say you're going to do something, you do it. I also learned early on that you should be the first person there (whether it's at work, at practice, etc.) and the last person to leave. I've never forgotten that. Even today, you'll find my car parked at our building early and you'll still see it until late. I've always believed that talk is cheap and that actions really do speak louder than words.

Now here is an example of Candace's brand exercise:

Her Strengths:

- Creativity
- Organization
- Crystal-clear communication

Her Passions:

- Helping people think differently about their lives and careers

- Helping people thrive and enjoy their work, no matter what they do

- Helping people communicate more clearly and consistently

Her Values:

- Delivering my best work, on time, all the time

- Being honest in my business dealings, treating people fairly, and generally being a good person

She also has brand mottos: *Do good work; don't be mean.* And *Trust first, so others will open up and trust you. You are only as good as the work you deliver.*

Candace's brand statement:

"I am a clear and organized communicator dedicated to consistently excellent work and fair and ethical business dealings. That's important because I'm a gig worker and contractor, which means I'm also a business brand. In my coaching, my job is to help people think creatively about their careers."

That sounds like a powerful brand statement.

Now it's your turn.

Identify at least three areas where you believe you show excellence—these would be your "Strengths."

Your Strengths:

_____

_____

Now identify three areas of work/life that you are particularly passionate about. You don't have to think too hard about these. They'll come right to the surface as soon as you think about what you care most about. These are your "Passions."

Your Passions:

_____

_____

Now list a couple of your most treasured values—these are usually core to who you are and how you live your life. You may even have a "motto" like Candace does. List your "Values" here.

Your Values:

_____

_____

Gina Rudan writes that "Identifying your genius means consciously acknowledging and taking active responsibility for your unique strengths, skills, expertise, passions, creativity, and values. Hint: the intersection of these quantitative and qualitative characteristics is where your practical genius lies."[7]

MIRRORSET
SELF-ASSESSMENT

Y ou made it! You've gone through twelve weeks of transformation, including some of the hardest work of all: changing your
image and the way people see you in your work life.

If you've completed the assessments and exercises along the way,
you should already be feeling more confident. Let's review the progress
you've made and what kind of feedback you're getting.

On a scale of 1 to 5, with 1 being the least true and 5 being the truest,
how would you rate yourself after four weeks of working on managing
your image and brand?

I have made changes to my body language and non-verbal communication skills that improve my interactions with people.

      1   **2**   **3**   **4**   **5**

List the changes you've made here.

- _____
- _____
- _____

I have made changes to my wardrobe, personal style, and/or technology that make me appear more stylish and/or more confident.

| 1 | 2 | 3 | 4 | 5 |

List the changes you've made here.

- _____
- _____
- _____

What would you still like to improve?

- _____
- _____
- _____

I have been getting more positive feedback on my appearance from family, friends, coworkers (maybe even strangers!).

| 1 | 2 | 3 | 4 | 5 |

I have worked on making a more positive first impression.

| 1 | 2 | 3 | 4 | 5 |

List the changes you've made here.

- _____
- _____
- _____

I am acting and performing my work more consistently and authentically.

| 1 | 2 | 3 | 4 | 5 |

List the changes you've made here.

- _____
- _____
- _____

I have started following thought leaders and innovative thinkers.

☐ Yes

☐ No

☐ Still working on it.

If yes, who have you started following and why do you think they're making an impression on your thinking?

- _____
- _____
- _____

I have created a brand statement.

☐ Yes

☐ No

☐ Still working on it.

☐ Not sure I can do this.

What words did you choose for your brand statement?

- _____

- _____

- _____

Even if you haven't developed a personal brand statement, have you changed the way you introduce yourself to people or explain what you do?

☐ Yes

☐ No

☐ Still working on it.

☐ Not sure I can do this.

What was the hardest change to make?

_____

_____

Why do you think that was?

_____

_____

For more help on developing your brand statement or elevator speech, find our free downloadable coaching guide at chrisflakus.com.

CONCLUSION

STAYING RELEVANT

Twelve weeks ago, we started this book together. Maybe you flew through it in a few weeks. Maybe it's taken a year. No matter how long it's taken you to get through it, I want you to pause for a moment and think about the changes you've made. You picked up this book because you were tired of feeling stuck, passed over for promotions, unable to move on to a better job, or simply disconnected from your colleagues. How has your life changed?

We also asked you in the Introduction: Would you hire you? I want to ask you the same question today. If I've done my job, the answer is YES!

No excuses! No lengthy reasons why you're not fitting in, getting hired, or being promoted. You know now you have what it takes to be relevant—not just now, but forever. The reality is that even as we wrote this book the workplace continued to change. Yes, the workplace is currently made up of Boomers, Gen X, Xennials, Millennials, and Gen Z—and Alphas have recently begun joining the ranks.

Artificial Intelligence (AI) is everywhere in nearly every industry. New industries are burgeoning; old ones are folding. Everything changes all the time, and will continue to. There are new songs, slang words, and popular social media platforms. There is always going to be the "new, latest, greatest" book, movie, television, or restaurant. You have no choice but to keep up.

You came to us because you wanted to get unstuck, and not feel limited by your age, your style, your experience—or the stories you told yourself. In essence, you wanted to age-proof your career by adopting the mindsets, skillsets, and what we call mirrorsets that developed you from the inside out. You've done the work. Now it's time to put all you learned into action.

By now you know you're COACHABLE. Congratulations, this might be your most winning asset. You will be relevant everywhere—at any time. No employee is more valuable than the one who is always looking to grow, learn, and listen to what others have to say. You will always be relevant if you can remain coachable. If you're looking for a coach—to keep this up—and to help you achieve any number of personal goals, head over to our website (chrisflakus.com) to look at our list of resources.

You're also ADAPTABLE. Again, nothing says: "I'm relevant!" like the ability to change when circumstances arise that demand you do.

You're also CURIOUS. By now you've shown an openness to admit you might be wrong or there might be a better way. Just by completing this book to the end you have demonstrated your curiosity. This too will keep you relevant forever. Never stop asking questions, never stop learning as much as you can about what others are interested in and curious about, and never, ever, assume there is nothing more to learn. There is always so much more to discover.

If you made it this far and filled out the Mindset, Skillset, and Mirrorset assessments, chances are you could give a master class of your own in receiving and applying feedback and constructive criticism. The ability to receive feedback and apply it is the secret sauce of staying relevant. If you are brave enough to ask for it, humble enough to receive it, and strong enough to apply it—you will always be relevant.

By now you also have a deep understanding of your VALUES, your BRAND, and your STORY—and you also understand that these will evolve over time. What you value today may change, as will your brand and your story. To stay relevant, I recommend reviewing these annually—especially if you are going through major life changes, career shifts, promotions, or starting over in some personal or professional way. It's so important to check in and assess where you have been, where you are, and where you want to go. Life is always changing, and so that means you have to change too.

Don't forget to keep honing your skills—EXCELLENCE will never be out of style. If you can do anything exceptionally well, you will immediately stand out. Again, a coach will be helpful, but so too will classes, workshops, retreats, certificate programs, and professional development. Don't underestimate the power of reading, either. Read or listen to books, audiobooks, or podcasts related to your career. Follow interesting bloggers and writers both inside and outside your industry. Stay up-to-date on changes in your field, and you'll always be relevant.

And last but not least—have FUN! Have a sense of humor about all this. Of course, it's not easy to change, but it helps to do so with a cheerful attitude. Being able to laugh at yourself and recognize your own foibles is the key to authenticity. You don't have to pretend to be someone you're not. Be yourself, own your mistakes and missteps, laugh a little bit at yourself for not knowing then what you do now, and move on. Don't let past mistakes keep you from taking the necessary steps that your Future Self will thank you for!

OUR HOPE FOR YOU

When Candace and I started working on this book together, we realized that collectively we had helped thousands of job seekers access training and build meaningful careers. But we knew we could be doing so much more. Not everyone has the means to hire a coach, and we wanted to put this information in the hands of as many people as possible. Our hope is that by reading this book you have gained a new mindset, skillset, and what we call "mirrorset" that will set you up for success and for life.

You had to do some tough introspection, but by now you should have a better understanding of yourself and your work. You have a new story to tell. Remember when we mentioned the baseball coach who said all coaching came down to looking at players and asking yourself: "What story does this guy wish someone would tell him about himself? And then you told the guy that story." I hope by now you can tell that story about yourself. You know the story you want for yourself—now, three years from now, and ten years from now. You know who you are and who you are meant to be. You aren't going to succumb at the hint of change, political shift, any recession, layoffs, economic downturns, or industry disruptions, health or family changes—because you know that whatever comes you'll be prepared. You're going to handle it. By becoming RELEVANT—you have become timeless. No matter what happens today, tomorrow, a month from now, or a year from now, you have the tools to take the next step and make the necessary changes.

We applaud your reinvention. And you should too! Celebrate! You've written a new story, a new future, a new you. And this deserves a moment of praise. Congratulate yourself for doing the work. Part of being relevant is pausing to take it all in—being present and taking time to revel in the wins. You've done so much and come so far—not just in the past twelve weeks, but in your career—so honor that. Be proud of the person you are and the person you're becoming. I promise that when you hold your head up with pride and with a smile on your face, you will be magnetic. It is so simple, but so powerful—show people who you are: confident, happy, joyful, and willing to do the work. You'll be amazed at how far this goes. It's so simple, but it works every time. When you're doing something that aligns with your goals and values, work doesn't have to be something you need to get through and get over as soon as possible. Instead of dreading Mondays, I hope you begin to look forward to them as a new day, a new opportunity to be with others and in service to others—and to demonstrate your purpose and value in the world. Because you matter. Your work matters. And the world needs you—and your skills, talents, and ideas.

You are now and forever will be: RELEVANT.

LET'S KEEP IN TOUCH.

If you feel motivated today—terrific! Let's keep that momentum up. Find yourself an accountability partner or create a RELEVANT Club—where you get together with others to talk about what is current, trending, or coming down the pipeline in your industry. Find a fun place to meet and share your ideas. Feel free to reach out to us and let us know if you do! If you experience some wins after implementing any of our recommendations, we want to hear about it. Share on Instagram, Facebook, or LinkedIn.

RESOURCES

MINDSET

If you're ready to start looking for new work or need a recruitment agency—feel free to reach out to CSI Companies at csicompanies.com

NEED COACHING?

Dr. Angela Love: Angelalove.com

SKILLSET

Some of the top online platforms for learning business working skills include: LinkedIn Learning, Coursera, Udemy, Skillshare, Simplilearn, and EdX. Each offers a range of courses focused on professional development, with strengths in different areas like industry-specific content, university-level instruction, diverse course variety, and creative skill development.

Key points about each platform:

- LinkedIn Learning: Excellent for career-oriented skills directly relevant to your LinkedIn profile, with a strong focus on professional development.

- Coursera: Provides access to high-quality courses from top universities and companies, ideal for those seeking structured learning with a potential for certificates or degrees.

- Udemy: A vast library of courses with diverse instructors, often at affordable prices, suitable for finding specific skills or niche topics.

- Skillshare: Focuses on creative and design-related skills, with a project-based learning approach.

- Simplilearn: Offers comprehensive business skill development programs with industry certifications, particularly for technical and management roles.

- EdX: Another platform with university-level courses, often featuring collaborative learning opportunities.

MIRRORSET

Headshot Software using AI: instaheadshots.com

Customized Wardrobe Sites to Help You Stay Relevant

- Daily Look: Dailylook.com

- Stitch Fix: Stitchfix.com

- Stately: Statelymen.com

Keeping Your Communication Relevant— Check Out These Apps:

- Grammarly.com
- Prowritingaid.com
- Ginger
- QueText
- CopyLeaks
- Writer
- Sapling
- Paper Rater
- Reverso
- Slick Write
- Hemingway
- ChatGPT
- Copilot

ACKNOWLEDGMENTS

From Chris: The idea for this book came from countless interactions with people at various places in their careers. After years of one-on-one meetings, I came to realize there were themes in people's struggles to find work and remain relevant, and I felt like this book could be a resource for many people who feel stuck in their careers.

Deciding to write a book is one thing—actually following through with it is another. I'd like to acknowledge and recognize those people who helped me in my career and stuck with me during both the good and challenging times. First, my wife Jennifer, who has been cheering me on throughout our lives together . . . celebrating the good times and helping me through the bad. To my kids for being patient and understanding about my long work weeks and business travel. To my CSI team and especially Kate Mays—you've made all the challenges worth it. To Rob Zandbergen and our RECRUIT leadership—thank you for your support.

When I look back at the thirty years of my career, I'm filled with gratitude for the people who took a chance on me. I would not have had the career I've been blessed to have without the support of my parents and siblings and I wouldn't be here without Delores Kesler, Guy

Cuddihee, Deborah Pass, Eric Stevens, and Don Langmo. I'm thankful for the opportunities you gave me, and I praise God that I took those opportunities seriously.

• • •

From Candace: I am grateful for my husband Thom's military career, which forced me to move around the country—and the world—and gave me the chance to reinvent myself in each new place we landed. He's been incredibly supportive of every stage of my career and my writing.

I have been fortunate to spend most of my professional career working in organizations dedicated to helping people make career transitions and find meaningful work. This is the book I've always wanted to write, and I hope it makes a difference for everyone who is brave enough to take on the hard work of self-reflection and change.

NOTES

INTRODUCTION: WOULD YOU HIRE YOU?

1. Chad Harbach, *The Art of Fielding* (Little, Brown and Company, 2011).

MONTH ONE: MINDSET PRACTICES

1. Carol Dweck, *Mindset: The New Psychology of Success* (Random House Publishing Group, 2006).
2. Sheryl Sandberg, *Lean In: Women, Work, and the Will to Lead* (Knopf Doubleday Publishing Group, 2013).
3. Pattie Sellers quoted in Sheryl Sandberg, *Lean In: Women, Work, and the Will to Lead* (Knopf Doubleday Publishing Group, 2013), 53.

WEEK 1: BE COACHABLE

1. Seth Godin, "Seth Godin's Freelancer Course," last updated April 2019, Udemy, https://www.udemy.com/course/seth-godin-freelancer-course/.

WEEK 2: BE ADAPTABLE

1. Seth Godin, "Working with Problems," *Seth's Blog*, November 18, 2023, https://seths.blog/2023/11/working-with-problems/.
2. Sheryl Sandberg and Adam Grant, *Option B: Facing Adversity, Building Resilience, and Finding Joy* (Knopf Doubleday Publishing Group, 2017).

WEEK 3: GET CURIOUS

1. *Ted Lasso*, season 1, episode 8, "The Diamond Dogs," directed by Declan Lowney, written by Jason Sudeikis, Bill Lawrence, and Brendan Hunt, featuring Jason Sudeikis, Hannah Waddingham, and Jeremy Swift, aired on September 18, 2020, on Apple TV, https://tv.apple.com/us/episode/the-diamond-dogs/umc.cmc.eaaizh8wdtnjuohaebw843ft?showId=umc.cmc.vtoh0mn0xn7t3c643xqonfzy&action=play.

WEEK 4: RECEIVING AND APPLYING FEEDBACK

1. *Prizzi's Honor*, directed by John Huston (1985; MGM Video, 2003), DVD.
2. GenWHY Communication Strategies, "Tips for Giving Feedback to Millennials and Generation Z," LinkedIn, July 17, 2023, https://www.linkedin.com/pulse/tips-giving-feedback-millennials-generation-z-genwhycommunications/.
3. Stephen Covey, *The Speed of Trust: The One Thing That Changes Everything* (Free Press, 2006), 13.

WEEK 5: IDENTIFY YOUR NEEDS, VALUES, EXPECTATIONS, AND NON-NEGOTIABLES

1. George Clooney, "George Clooney LEARN FROM FAILURE," posted by @EnergizedAgent, YouTube Short, February 21, 2024, https://www.youtube.com/shorts/7_-kQF0kvEw.

WEEK 6: BUILD A RECORD OF EXCELLENCE

1. Tessa White, *The Unspoken Truths for Career Success: Navigating Pay, Promotions, and Power at Work* (HarperCollins Leadership, 2023).
2. Emily Priddy, "The One Skill That Will Make Your Boss Wish They Had Ten of You," Simon Sinek's Optimism Company, March 20, 2024, https://simonsinek.com/stories/the-one-skill-that-will-make-your-boss-wish-they-had-ten-of-you/.
3. Lauren Comander, "Is AI Coming for Your Job? Not if You Embrace It," *FIU Business Now*, October 2, 2023, https://business.fiu.edu/news/2023/is-ai-coming-for-your-job.html.
4. "AI Certificate Course for Communicators," Ragan, accessed July 25, 2025, https://www.ragan.com/store/ai-certificate-course-for-communicators/.
5. Stephen King, *On Writing: A Memoir of the Craft* (Scribner, 2000).

WEEK 7: REFRAME YOUR STORY

1. Gene Combs and Jill Freedman, *Narrative Therapy: The Social Construction of Preferred Realities* (W. W. Norton & Company, 1996), 32.

2. Kaytee Gillis, "8 Common Dysfunctional Family Roles: Through Self-Awareness, We Can Work to Change Patterns We Took into Adulthood," *Psychology Today*, March 23, 2023, https://www.psychologytoday.com/us/blog/invisible-bruises/202303/8-common-dysfunctional-family-roles.

3. Regina Brett, "50 Lessons from *God Never Blinks* by Regina Brett," *Regina Brett* (blog), accessed July 25, 2025, https://www.reginabrett.com/50-life-lessons.

WEEK 8: SELF-AWARENESS ACTION PLAN

1. Mark Murphy, "Neuroscience Explains Why You Need to Write Down Your Goals If You Actually Want to Achieve Them," *Forbes*, April 15, 2018, https://www.forbes.com/sites/markmurphy/2018/04/15/neuroscience-explains-why-you-need-to-write-down-your-goals-if-you-actually-want-to-achieve-them/.

WEEK 9: MANAGING YOUR FIRST IMPRESSION

1. Jennifer K. South Palomares and Andrew W. Young, "Facial First Impressions of Partner Preference Traits: Trustworthiness, Status, and Attractiveness," *Social Psychological and Personality Science* 9, no. 8 (2017): 990-1000, https://doi.org/10.1177/1948550617732388.

2. Eric Dolan, "Study Reveals Just How Quickly We Form a First Impression," PsyPost, October 30, 2017, https://www.psypost.org/study-reveals-just-quickly-form-first-impression/.

3. Albert Mehrabian, *Silent Messages: Implicit Communication of Emotions and Attitudes* (Wadsworth Publishing Company, 1981), 76.

4. Vanessa Friedman, "I'm Moving to a New City. Do I Have to Change the Way I Dress?," Ask Vanessa, *New York Times*, June 17, 2024, https://www.nytimes.com/2024/06/17/style/moving-style-new-city.html.

5. Friedman, "I'm Moving to a New City. Do I Have to Change the Way I Dress?"

6. Friedman, "I'm Moving to a New City. Do I Have to Change the Way I Dress?"

7. Rob LaZebnik, "It's True: You Talk Too Much: How to Achieve the Optimal 50-50 Conversation Flow," *Wall Street Journal*, October 4, 2013, https://www.wsj.com/articles/it8217s-true-you-talk-too-much-1380909929.

WEEK 10: HOW TO BE AUTHENTIC AND STAY RELEVANT

1. *Merriam-Webster*, s.v. "authentic (*adjective*)," accessed July 25, 2025, https://www. merriam-webster.com/dictionary/authentic.

2. Lisa Rosh and Lynn Offermann, "Be Yourself, but Carefully," *Harvard Business Review*, October 2013, https://hbr.org/2013/10/be-yourself-but-carefully.

3. Rosh and Offermann, "Be Yourself, but Carefully."

4. Rosh and Offermann, "Be Yourself, but Carefully."

5. Rosh and Offermann, "Be Yourself, but Carefully."

6. Liz Kislik, "Why People Lie at Work and What to Do About It," *Harvard Business Review*, June 2021, https://hbr.org/2021/06/why-people-lie-at-work-and-what-to-do-about-it.

7. *The Naked Jungle*, directed by Byron Haskin (1954; Paramount, 2004), DVD.

WEEK 11: CULTURE COUNTS

1. Glassdoor, "88% of Employees Consider Culture Important to Overall Satisfaction," Glassdoor Recruiting Website, accessed December 4, 2024, https:// www.glassdoor.com.

2. Deloitte, "94% of Executives Believe Culture Is a Main Driver of Business Success," Deloitte Survey, accessed December 4, 2024, https://www2.deloitte.com.

WEEK 12: MASTERING YOUR PERSONAL BRAND

1. Jill Avery and Rachel Greenwald, "A New Approach to Building Your Personal Brand," *Harvard Business Review*, May-June 2023, https://hbr.org/2023/05/a-new-approach-to-building-your-personal-brand.

2. Avery and Greenwald, "A New Approach."

3. Avery and Greenwald, "A New Approach."

4. Avery and Greenwald, "A New Approach."

5. Kevin Carroll, "Foreword," in Gina Amaro Rudan, *Practical Genius: A 5-Step Plan to Turn Your Talent and Passion into Success* (Touchstone, 2011), ix.

6. Rudan, *Practical Genius*, 15.

7. Rudan, *Practical Genius*, 19.

ABOUT THE AUTHORS

CHRIS FLAKUS, an award-winning executive with over three decades of distinguished leadership in the workforce solutions and staffing industry, is the visionary force behind the extraordinary growth of CSI Companies. As chief executive officer since 2020 and a board member, having previously served as president since 2003, Chris has driven a remarkable fifty-fold increase in revenue and EBITDA, solidifying CSI's leadership in the industry.

An alumnus of the University of North Florida, Chris began his career as a recruiter, rapidly advancing through sales and leadership roles to become a transformative figure in the staffing sector. His strategic acumen and deep industry insight have consistently delivered innovative solutions. For over a decade, he personally spearheaded executive searches, successfully placing hundreds of professionals in high-impact roles with annual compensation ranging from $75,000 to $500,000.

Chris's leadership has driven unparalleled financial success while cultivating a resilient, innovative corporate culture that positions CSI Companies for sustained excellence. Renowned for his ability to navigate complex market dynamics, he continues to shape the future of workforce solutions.

Chris resides in Jacksonville, Florida, with his wife and children.

CANDACE MOODY is a writer with over twenty-five years of experience in career coaching and workforce development. She wrote features and an employment column for the *Florida Times-Union* from 2007–2018, and her writing on the workplace has been featured in the *Jacksonville Business Journal*. During her workforce development career, she was frequently interviewed by the media on employment issues.

She is also an award-winning blogger and speaker who taught a class in executive communication skills at Jacksonville University's Davis School of Business from 2012–2019. Candace's writing can be found on her Authory site, www.authory.com/CandaceMoody, and at her website, www.candacemoody.com. She lives with her husband in Jacksonville, Florida.